T0328692

Cambridge Elements ≡

Elements in Corporate Governance
edited by
Thomas Clarke
UTS Business School, University of Technology Sydney

THE ROLE OF THE BOARD IN CORPORATE PURPOSE AND STRATEGY

Robert Bood
Tilburg University

Hans van Ees
University of Groningen

Theo Postma
University of Groningen

CAMBRIDGE
UNIVERSITY PRESS

Shaftesbury Road, Cambridge CB2 8EA, United Kingdom

One Liberty Plaza, 20th Floor, New York, NY 10006, USA

477 Williamstown Road, Port Melbourne, VIC 3207, Australia

314–321, 3rd Floor, Plot 3, Splendor Forum, Jasola District Centre,
New Delhi – 110025, India

103 Penang Road, #05–06/07, Visioncrest Commercial, Singapore 238467

Cambridge University Press is part of Cambridge University Press & Assessment,
a department of the University of Cambridge.

We share the University's mission to contribute to society through the pursuit of
education, learning and research at the highest international levels of excellence.

www.cambridge.org
Information on this title: www.cambridge.org/9781009221085

DOI: 10.1017/9781009221092

First published 2022

A catalogue record for this publication is available from the British Library.

ISBN 978-1-009-22108-5 Paperback
ISSN 2515-7175 (online)
ISSN 2515-7167 (print)

The Role of the Board in Corporate Purpose and Strategy

Elements in Corporate Governance

DOI: 10.1017/9781009221092
First published online: August 2022

Robert Bood
Tilburg University

Hans van Ees
University of Groningen

Theo Postma
University of Groningen

Author for correspondence: Hans van Ees, h.van.ees@rug.nl

Abstract: This Element is an attempt to contribute to the extant literature on boards and corporate governance by exploring in detail the active involvement of the board in the purpose and strategy of the corporation in order to cope with a complex and uncertain environment.

Keywords: corporate governance, board of directors, corporate strategy, corporate purpose, uncertainty and complexity

ISBNs: 9781009221085 (PB), 9781009221092 (OC)
ISSNs: 2515-7175 (online), 2515-7167 (print)

Contents

1 Introduction

The global system dynamics of the twenty-first century are in marked contrast with the relative stability of the second half of the previous century (Guillen and Ontiveros, 2016). A global pandemic, global warming, global financial and economic crises, global political fragmentation, global migration and global income inequality, all are recognised as tipping points that threaten the sustainability of society. Moreover, disruptive technologies, e.g. robotics, digitisation and biotechnology, are fundamentally affecting the nature of production, communication and interaction in society. The belief that the world is changing fast, and that such changes may have important yet uncertain implications, is widespread.

Embedded in the global dynamics is a changing perspective on the nature and roles of corporations in society. First, while technological developments allow the unbundling of production processes and structures, for instance, the recent pandemic has also revealed the vulnerability of global value chains and led to calls for a shortening of Supply chains to improve resilience even at the expense of efficiency and competitiveness. Second, global environmental degradation has created (in line with first, third, fourth) concerns about the purpose and distribution of value created in corporations as being too exclusively focused on short-term economic returns. Third, the global economic crisis has challenged the legitimacy and trustworthiness of financial corporations in particular. And fourth, the increasing world income and wealth inequality raised questions as to the humanitarian effects of global sourcing, the massive scale of operations and the concentration of ownership and decision rights within corporations (Davis, 2016). The resulting decline in trust is further fuelled by corporate scandals in banks, automobile companies, the clothing industry, energy, food, pharmaceuticals and so on. Finally, the Panama and Paradise Papers have revealed corporate activities that are widely perceived as unfair and unethical. For some, these developments indicate 'the end of capitalism' and that 'firms need a purpose far more inspiring than merely maximising shareholder value' (Raworth, 2017: 89).

Corporate governance concerns institutions that create and allocate power and influence over decision-making about the control and direction of the corporation (Aguilera and Jackson, 2010). Essentially, corporate governance represents the answer to two related questions. The first question is for whom the organisation creates value, and the second is who holds the ultimate decision rights. It is precisely the answers to these two questions that are challenged by the global developments mentioned in the previous paragraph. Traditionally, corporate governance addresses both questions by assigning ultimate decision rights and responsibilities (i.e. decision-making authority) to actors within the corporation that have a residual claim on the value created in the organisation (Monks and Minow, 2004). Identifying shareholders as the only residual claimants in today's world, good corporate governance has been judged by the way in which shareholder interests are best served. In recent decades, multiple best practices have emerged suggesting a preferred composition of boards, audits and risk- and remuneration-management systems. Numerous discussions on good corporate governance have followed referring to the effectiveness of such mechanisms. Problematic with this approach is that increased asset specialisation and recognition of other interests may imply the presence of multiple stakeholders besides shareholders with such residual claims (Rajan and Zingales, 1998). And notwithstanding best practices, current corporate governance – with its emphasis on distrust and control – has not been effective in (re-)establishing societal trust in the corporate sector (Boivie et al., 2016). Corporations across the globe are continually struggling with major uncertainties, appropriate governance structures, relationships to stakeholders and society and even their purpose as a corporation.

Examples such as big mining, big tech and fossil energy corporations suggest that, in tandem with the business environment, the nature of the firm itself is changing. Knowledge capital, tacit knowledge and intangible assets are more relevant nowadays than physical, tangible assets. Boundaries of the firm fade, networks abound (Zingales, 2000). Corporate agility, attention to strategic risk, changing business models, co-creation, emergence and fundamental uncertainties are essential to understanding corporate success and corporations that are struggling to adapt to modern times. What applies to corporations in general applies to the board of directors in particular. Board activity is involvement in strategy (cf. Andrews, 1980: 95, 170–6). However, the paradigm of the separation of decision management and control (Fama and Jensen, 1983) has degraded this involvement to a focus on ratifying decisions, risk management and control, symbolic compliance to codes and transparency of the annual report. Despite calls for a more holistic perspective, the narrow view of corporate finance, with a primary focus on the relationship between the corporation and the shareholder, paying only lip service to stakeholder dialogue and culture, may still reign in the boardroom (Business Roundtable, 2018, 2019).

In this Element, it is argued that the global dynamics call for a revitalised perspective on the role of the board in the corporate purpose and strategy of the firm. Among others, the need emerges from the inability of companies to exercise control in the current complex world they currently operate in. Without effective control, less control-dependent modes of collaboration in value creation are worth examining. Value-creating boards are characterised by an active working style, strategic engagement of directors and ability to balance exploitation and exploration (Huse, 2007; Van Ees, Bood and Postma, 2019). In particular, the role of the board is to actively work on safeguarding ambidexterity, to cherish network connections with stakeholders and to give meaning to corporate citizenship; to facilitate experimentation and explore opportunities and capabilities, while simultaneously improving current operations and nourishing decisions that stretch current mental models; and to contribute to strategy by challenging core assumptions and shaping the purpose and agenda of management for the future sustainability of the corporation. This call for strategic engagement indicates that the board must go beyond their traditional roles of control and monitoring, service and resource provision. The Element is an attempt to contribute to the extant literature of boards and corporate governance to explore in detail such active involvement of the board in purpose and strategy to cope with the complex and uncertain environment.

2 The Nature of the Firm

2.1 The Nature of the Corporation

The corporation can be regarded as a network of firm-specific knowledge investments of multiple stakeholders. Combining these investments, corporations produce synergistic value that cannot be realised through market exchanges (Rajan and Zingales, 1998). Mayer, Wright and Phan (2017) identify three generic challenges for this joint value creation within corporations. First, the value creation of corporations is shifting from being based on tangible assets to being based on intangible assets. The emphasis on intangible assets and mutual firm-specific investments by human beings can only imperfectly be managed through formal contract and requires, moreover, reliance on trust-based relationships. Second, next to production, formal contracting is complicated by the accountability structure, which is becoming increasingly complex as social pressure and environmental concerns result in a fundamental reconsideration of the position of the corporation in society. Corporations are held accountable against a larger diversity of (private and public) needs across the globe, by both internal and external stakeholders, and hence their increased contribution to addressing social needs and providing (semi-)public goods and services in different segments of the world. Third, stakeholder networks make the boundaries of corporations fade. Corporate value creation requires the active involvement and engagement of multiple internal and external stakeholders. Corporations need to effectively navigate relationships, norms, rules and routines to enable effective collaboration, exchange information, enhance predictability and establish legitimacy. The corporation needs to handle not only the content but also the emerging context of multiple stakeholder relationships, which defines the corporation primarily as a social institution next to an economic entity. Firm-specific investments by stakeholders cause sunk costs once contracts have been concluded. As these firm-specific investments have a much lower value outside the firm, the ex post bargaining position of stakeholders is weakened when the quasi-rents are divided. Thus, corporations constitute the multilateral agreements and institutional arrangements for governing relationships between sets of stakeholders that contribute firm-specific assets to the firm value creation. The corporation can be regarded as a network of relationships among internal and external stakeholders contributing to joint value creation through firm-specific tangible and intangible stakeholder investments (Bridoux and Stoelhorst, 2014); hence, the corporation cannot only or primarily be regarded as a bundle of assets, it is also very much a community of people, of human beings who participate in relationships that are meaningful and valuable to them.

2.2 The Purpose of the Corporation

Thus, to ensure stakeholder commitment and stewardship and to navigate relationships, corporations need to be clear about the purpose of their value-creating activities. Over the last decades, the perception of the ultimate objective of corporate value creation has been shifting from profits to operational excellence and from customer satisfaction to more existential contributions to society. In this perspective, the corporate purpose represents the meaning-rich articulation of the main business of the firm, the firm's reason for existence. Bartlett and Ghoshal (1994: 88) define purpose as 'the statement of a company's moral response to its broadly defined responsibilities, not an amoral plan for exploiting commercial opportunity'. Thakor and Quinn (2013: 2) similarly define it as 'something that is perceived as producing a social benefit over and above the tangible pecuniary payoff that is shared by the principal and the agent'. Purpose focuses on the corporation as a whole and defines the corporation's reason for being there. A well-defined corporate purpose triggers engagement and commitment of stakeholders. Needless to say that a strong identification with purpose by all stakeholders cannot be derived from profit maximisation only, simply because profit generally represents the benefit to only one of the stakeholder groups, i.e. the shareholders. In this respect, Freeman, Phillips and Sisodia (2020) argue that profit maximisation 'as its implicit or explicit purpose will soon find stakeholders operating at cross-purposes. It sets them up as adversarial claimants on what is seen as a limited pool of available profit in the system' (220). Thus, corporate purpose reflects the stakeholders' shared beliefs about the meaning of a firm's activities beyond one-dimensional measures of performance (Gartenberg, Prat and Serfeim 2019) – this despite heterogeneous stakeholder interests, needs and preferences. The collectively determined corporate purpose defines why the organisation exists and serves to attract and hold stakeholders and foster stakeholder commitment. Purpose gives meaning to their contributions and serves to identify with the organisation. A strong identification with the corporate purpose changes stakeholders into stewards. Argenti (1980) even speaks of 'intended beneficiaries', who should be involved in deciding about the ultimate objective, as the concept that validates the entire organisation and every action it takes.

2.3 The Nature of Corporate Decision-Making

Despite the emphasis on corporate decision-making and the distribution of decision-making authority, the actual practice of decision-making has only received scant attention. By contrast, in the seminal work *A Behavioral Theory of the Firm*, the development and understanding of organisational behaviour and decision-making is the key objective (Simon 1945, 1955; March and Simon, 1958; Cyert and March, 1963). Juxtapositioning the mainstream rationality paradigm, the behavioural theory of the firm is built around the well-known key concepts of bounded rationality, satisficing and problemistic search, the routinisation of decision-making in standard operating procedures and the dominant coalition (Argote and Greve, 2007). We will shortly introduce these concepts before discussing their implications for theory development regarding the role of boards in corporate purpose and strategy (see also Van Ees, Gabrielsson and Huse, 2009).

2.3.1 Bounded Rationality

Bounded rationality refers to the notion that decision makers in organisations experience limits in their ability to process information and solve complex problems (Simon, 1955; March and Simon, 1958; Cyert and March, 1963). The complexity of the business environment and cognitive limitations make it impossible to completely identify and understand all linkages among variables and de facto renders the application of rationality principles to decision-making impossible. Recognising complexity thus may imply simplifying decision rules, such as those embodied by strategic planning and control and trial and error. Bounded rationality implies that actors are unable to maximise value given the constraints on their decision-making capabilities. In addition, a behavioural approach may also include such factors as cognitive biases and incompetence as explanations for inefficient and ineffective decision-making (Foss, 2001; Hendry, 2005). In a complex environment, limited and biased cognitions of organisational actors only allow for an imperfect mapping of the decision-making environment and limited, imprecise and selective information processing, which increase uncertainty as defined as the gap between available and needed information to perform a task (Galbraith, 1973). From this perspective, the limited competence and awareness among an organisation's members may represent a much more likely cause of organisational inefficiencies and failure than opportunism, which assumes that individuals have a full understanding of the opportunities available to them (Hendry, 2005).

2.3.2 Satisficing Behaviour and Problemistic Search

A second key concept is satisficing behaviour, implying that actors tend to accept choices or judgements that are 'good enough', based on their most important current needs, rather than searching for optimal solutions. Decisions are not optimal solutions to problems but reflect solutions that satisfy particular aspiration levels (Cyert and March, 1963; see also Levinthal and March, 1993). Aspiration levels may reflect the corporate purpose, determined as a function of the organisation's past performance, benchmarked against other organisations and resulting in negotiating processes between main (coalitions of) actors; through specifying their requirements in terms of aspiration levels in the form of attainable goals, rather than constraints, aspiration levels can be seen as institutionalised indicators of the purpose of the firm (cf. Cyert and March, 1959).

The notion of satisficing behaviour rests on the observation that decision makers are primarily concerned with immediate problems and short-run solutions, something which has generally been referred to as 'problemistic search' (March and Simon, 1958; Cyert and March, 1963); this might contribute to a 'felt need for joint decision making', to forgo 'difference in goals (perceptions) and ultimate intergroup conflict with respect to the purpose' (March and Simon, 1958: 149). Problems are recognised to the extent that an organisation has failed to satisfy one or more of its self-imposed aspiration levels, or when such failure can be expected in the near future (Cyert and March, 1963). Problem recognition itself is primarily driven by attention allocation and selection biases. When faced with a purpose gap, decision makers can therefore be expected to search for solutions using simple heuristics or decision-making routines. The problem is regarded as solved as soon as an alternative is found that satisfies current objectives, or when goals have been revised to a level that makes available solutions acceptable through adjustment of aspiration as an actor's indicator of the firm's objective attainment. Decision-making is consequently seen as a process in which a corporation adapts to its changing environment through learning and experimentation.

2.3.3 Routinisation of Decision-Making

A third key concept is decision-making on the basis of 'routines' that are built up over time (Ocasio, 1999; Zahra and Filatotchev, 2004). Routines are performance programmes (March and Simon, 1958) or standard operating procedures (Cyert and March, 1963) and can be understood as the codified memory of the organisation, embodying the past experience, knowledge, beliefs, values and capabilities of the organisation and its decision makers (March and Simon, 1958; Cyert and March, 1963). Routines consist largely of experiential knowledge, which may be tacit and hard to codify. Routines store and reproduce experientially acquired competences, which can then be repeated over time.

Routines contribute to control and stability and both enable and constrain organisational action. On the one hand, routines conserve the cognitive abilities of decisionmakers and serve to channel and limit conflict among them. On the other hand, they direct attention to selected aspects of identified problem situations (Cyert and March, 1963). Rules and routines are hence not purely passive elements; rather, they serve as socially and historically constructed programs of action that direct attention to selected aspects of a problem situation. As such, they also create decision-making biases. Decision makers, however, are not victims of history; routines can be changed by learning processes, such as through imitation or through trial and error. Thus, both routinisation and unlearning play a central role in a behavioural-theory framework. This makes relying on a decision maker's experience and reasoning by analogy particularly problematic.

2.3.4 Political Bargaining in the Context of Corporations as Coalitions of Stakeholders

A fourth key concept from *A Behavioral Theory of the Firm* is political bargaining in the context of the firm as a coalition of stakeholders (Pearce, 1995; Huse and Rindova, 2001). Political bargaining depicts the organisation as a complex socio-political system with agents organised in coalitions (March, 1962; Cyert and March, 1963). To some degree, coalition partners may have distinct preferences and objectives, which make deliberation, negotiation and bargaining among coalitions common practice. Shifting coalitions of organisational actors affect purpose enactment and organisational decisions. Interest alignment is created through bargaining rather than through incentives. Disagreement about purpose enactment is dealt with in the context of ongoing bargaining processes among coalitions that pursue alternative objectives and priorities. Different coalitions may pursue conflicting objectives, and organisations may encompass a variety of possibly conflicting and inconsistent goals by pursuing them sequentially. Purpose is thus achieved through a series of routines and procedures, subject to local rationality and satisficing, as well as sequential attention to goals (Cyert and March, 1963). Its procedural rationality depends on the process that generated it (Simon, 1976: 131). It is recognised that this procedural rationality has a political or power component (e.g. Pettigrew, 1985). This is sometimes referred to as political rationality (e.g. Postma, 1989) and may result in thwarting the problem-solution process through the hierarchy of decision makers and the interests of different actors, a process related to the 'appropriate deliberation'. This means that in order to arrive at (sub)optimal rational decision-making, two components of rationality must be considered: the procedural and the political dimension (Bailey and Peck, 2013). This is especially the case for strategic decisions that concern the organisation as a whole and/or the firm's continuity. Strategic planning, with its focus on phases and different routines (see Section 3), is a good example of procedural rationality. Examples of political behaviour that may affect procedural rationality are offline lobbying, controlling agendas, withholding information, behind-the-scenes coalition forming and co-optation (Bailey and Peck, 2013).

Procedures for resolving conflicts do not necessarily lead to a consistent set of goals in the organisation. This means that organisations can most of the time be expected to have a considerable amount of latent conflicts and objectives. In this political context, the (re-)establishment of corporate purpose may serve to initiate deliberation towards agreement and consensus, trigger an additional search for information and knowledge or enhance societal legitimacy. In view of their formal role as 'the strategic apex' of the organisation, the board of directors will play an important role in these processes of purpose re-establishment and goal formation through creating shared mental models, visions, assumptions and belief structures, which inform their common expectations.

3 Strategy in a Complex and Uncertain Environment

3.1 Complexity and Uncertainty

Complexity in society emerges from populations of interacting actors. Each actor interacts situationally according to locally known rules, yet the dynamics of the social system can only be captured from the system as a whole (Arthur, 1999). Controlling the system at the actor level is impossible, the system can only be addressed from a holistic perspective. This applies to all open social systems, including corporations. To come to grips with the dynamics of the corporation in particular, three phenomena are relevant. First, emergence, the appearance of novel coherent structures out of self-organisation. Emergence can be managed through synchronisation and regulating interaction between actors. Second, transitions, unexpected changes in the state-space characteristics of the system. Transitions can be anticipated through early-warning signals, herding, nudging, requiring out-of-the-box thinking and the recognition of decision-making biases. Third, resilience, the ability to adapt to major shocks. To create resilience, buffers, institutions, regulation and diversity are among the options.

As mentioned in Section 1, the twenty-first-century business environment is emerging and transitioning both more rapidly and more radically as a result of the following mutually reinforcing developments. First, as the global economy has opened up, it has become more advanced and integrated, with more heterogeneous actors from different parts of the world competing intensively for the same opportunities as well as working together on innovative products and systems (Teece, Peteraf and Leih, 2016). Second, radical innovations and shocks are more readily transmitted and felt across the world. Globalisation of production technology has also led to independent, specialised suppliers, which, in combination with improvements in capital markets, have made physical assets less unique and outsourcing of production more common (Zingales, 2000). Third, intangible assets and tacit competences have become much more important than physical assets and are the foundation of many successful business models of this century (Mayer, 2016). Fourth, technological innovation has accelerated and become more intricately connected in integrated systems that require cooperation among a broad variety of partners in and across innovative ecosystems (Adner and Kapoor, 2010; Autio and Thomas, 2014). Fifth and finally, rather than within the boundaries of the firm, innovation occurs in a broader business and societal context of interdependent human relationships.

In the strategy literature, business environments have typically been described in terms of uncertainty, dynamism, volatility, complexity and ambiguity (see e.g. Miller and Friesen, 1983; Schoemaker, Heaton and Teece, 2018). Knight (1921) makes a distinction between risk and uncertainty. Whereas for risk the probabilities of possible outcomes are known, this information is lacking for uncertainty, as it, in general, concerns highly unique situations with 'unknown unknowns' that may unexpectedly present themselves (Teece, 2007). Koopmans (1957) refers to this as 'primary uncertainty' and distinguishes it from 'secondary uncertainty' that arises from a lack of communication between economic actors. Helfat and Teece (1987) broaden this definition by adopting Williamson's (1985) concept of 'behavioral uncertainty' to include unpredictable, opportunistic interactions between suppliers and buyers in the value chain. Vertical integration has proven effective in reducing secondary and behavioural uncertainty and was the preferred route of twentieth-century firms in more static business environments. When business environments are more dynamic, firms outsource activities and the boundaries between the firm and their business networks fade, secondary and behavioural uncertainties increase and have to be reduced in other ways.

Duncan (1972) considers the simple–complex and the static–dynamic dimensions as distinct aspects of uncertainty. The more complex the environment, the more heterogeneous factors and hence contingencies are involved. In more stable environments, contingencies remain by and large the same, whereas they are constantly changing in highly dynamic contexts (Davis, Eisenhardt and Bingham, 2009). The more complex and dynamic the environment, in general the higher the uncertainty. Mason and Mitroff (1981) add that the elements of complex environments are deeply interrelated. As a consequence, deviations emerging in one element are transmitted, magnified or modified to other elements, making state-space characteristics of environments greatly uncertain. Milliken (1987) emphasises that environmental uncertainty is in the eye of the beholder, as managers can be uncertain about the state of the environment making it unpredictable for them (state uncertainty). In addition, she notes that managers may be unable to predict what the impact of environmental changes will be on their organisation (effect uncertainty) or what options they have to respond to these changes and what the outcomes of these options are (respond uncertainty). This corresponds to the distinction Postma and Bood (2015) make between environmental uncertainty and the strategic uncertainty that results from it for firms with respect to impact and decision outcomes. Note that Koopmans' (1957) secondary uncertainty can enlarge strategic uncertainty for firms. Given the degree of environmental uncertainty, strategic uncertainty may also differ across firms depending on their dynamic capabilities or lack of it (Teece, Pisano and Shuen, 1997).

Environmental uncertainty ranges on a continuum from highly certain to highly uncertain. On the one hand, highly certain environments may be characterised by a low number of elements that are loosely connected and more static or subject to only incremental change. Situations may range from simple to complicated, with multiple risks of different kinds. However, as cause–effect relationships are known and the outcomes of possible responses can be identified, situations and risks can be assessed and managed through skillful analysis by well-educated experts (Snowden and Boone, 2007). On the other hand, highly uncertain environments are characterised by high complexity, with large numbers of heterogeneous factors interacting and changing continuously. As these tend to be unique and novel situations that have never been experienced before and contain 'unknown unknowns', cause–effect relationships are not clear, and both analysis and sense-making fall short. Even afterwards, there may be multiple interpretations of what has happened (Snowden and Boone, 2007). The type of uncertainty where multiple interpretations of the facts can be supported is known as 'equivocality' (Weick, 1979).

Most of the time, firms find themselves somewhere on a continuum between full certainty and complete uncertainty. Part of the future is already known and emerges from what has already happened. Next to critical uncertainties, the scenario literature distinguishes so-called predetermined elements (Wack, 1985; Van der Heijden, 1996). These are events and developments that have already occurred or started but whose consequences still have to unfold fully (an example is the recent Covid-19 pandemic). It is certain there will be effects, but it can be uncertain for a long time how and to what extent these will manifest themselves and what the implications for society, industries and firms will be. The present reveals some clues about future developments, but there is also, to a greater or lesser extent, environmental uncertainty, while corporate decision makers may face strategic uncertainty as they are partially unsure about strategic implications and effective responses. As March (1994: 178) puts it, corporate decision-making is surrounded by ambiguity as 'alternative states are hazily defined'.

The firm itself is a reflection of the complexity of society. Value creation is increasingly sourced in the context of trust-based relationships, multiple stakeholder orientations and coalitions and a reconsideration of corporate purpose that extends beyond formal corporate boundaries (Mayer, Wright and Phan, 2017). The firm itself emerges as a nexus of firm-specific knowledge investments by multiple stakeholders, and corporate decision-making structures follow suit (Grandori, 2016). Corporate strategy incorporates interdependent relationships, uncertain outcomes and conflicting views held by various stakeholders. As the boundaries of the firm are increasingly fading (Zingales, 2000), proactively shaping the broader business environment rather than merely adapting to it has become paramount for effective strategy (Teece, 2007; Autio and Thomas, 2014).

3.2 Perspectives on Strategy Making

The origins of strategic management go back to the 1950s, when Drucker (1954) and Selznick (1957) pointed to the key role leadership plays in shaping the future direction of their company based on the assessment of internal and external conditions. Their efforts were followed by Chandler's (1962) historical study into the success of America's largest corporations, which led to his assertion that 'structure follows strategy', which is still echoed today. Sloan (1963) confirmed the key role of the multidivisional structure in the success of General Motors' diversification strategy and emphasised the need to constantly anticipate and adapt to changing market conditions. The landmark textbooks written by Ansoff (1965), Ackoff (1970) and Andrews (1971) formalised the planning and design of corporate strategy and were leading in the strategic-management literature for several decades.

Since those pioneering publications, the literature on strategic manage-ment has expanded exponentially in breadth and depth. Overlooking decades of research and practices in strategic management, Hambrick and Fredrickson (2001: 49) conclude that 'strategy has become a catchall term used to mean whatever one wants it to mean'. Durand, Grand and Madsen (2017) call for integration of strategic-management research to mitigate the risk of growing incoherence and fragmentation in the field. Over the years, various typologies have been proposed to cover the wide plethora of per-spectives on strategy and strategy making. Chaffee (1985), for example, distinguishes between three modes of strategy that are implicit in the litera-ture: linear strategy focusing on sequential planning, adaptive strategy stres-sing the match between changing external and internal conditions and interpretive strategy springing from the social construction of reality. By classifying strategy approaches along the axes of strategy process (deliberate versus emergent) and outcomes (profit maximisation versus pluralistic), Whittington (1993) identifies four basic theories of strategy: classical (act rational), evolutionary (natural selection), processual (do it together) and systemic (embedded in higher-level systems). Mintzberg, Ahlstrand and Lampel (2009) classify the field of strategic management in no fewer than ten complementary schools that together are needed to obtain a complete picture of the content and process of strategy making. Some of these schools are more prescriptive (design, planning, positioning), while others are more descriptive in nature (entrepreneurial, cognitive, learning, power, cultural, environmental, configuration).

To explore the roles boards play in strategy in different kinds of environ-ments, we build upon the taxonomy of strategy approaches in Wiltbank et al. (2006), based on their review of the extant literature. By combining the degree of (assumed) environmental uncertainty and hence predictability and stability of environmental conditions in which organisations operate with the degree to which conditions can be controlled by organisations, they discern four distinct approaches to strategy making: planning, adaptive, visionary and

Table 1 Strategy-making in regimes of uncertainty and control

		Emphasis on control	
		Low	**High**
Emphasis on perceived uncertainty	High	Adapting & learning	Transforming & probing
	Low	Planning & positioning	Visioning & creating

The table above paraphrases Wiltbank et al. (2006: 983)

transformative (see Table 1). Whereas the first two approaches see the environment as exogenous to and imposed on organisations, the latter two consider it as endogenous and, to a greater or lesser extent, malleable by organisations. In line with this, the planning and adaptive schools rely heavily on either thorough external analysis to build better models of the outside world or high flexibility to respond as best as possible to rapid external changes when these occur. In the visionary and transformative schools, decisions and actions are informed by socially constructed realities, which only exist inside the human mind and are not considered to be reproductions of an external world. The four approaches also reflect the evolution of strategic-management thinking and practice over time in response to increasing environmental complexity and increasing interaction between organisations. In the following sections, we will explore the four approaches as distinguished by Wiltbank et al. (2006) in the context of the role of the board in strategy and purpose.

Like Mintzberg, Ahlstrand and Lampel (2009), we consider these four approaches as complementary alternative perspectives on the process of strategy making that can, separately and simultaneously, inform boards on appropriate approaches to strategy making depending on circumstances and preferences. Planning and visioning approaches both match with conditions in which environmental uncertainty is assumed to be low, with the former reducing any possible strategic uncertainty by detailed programming and the latter through the powerful messaging of an inspiring vision. While the relevance of adapting and transforming approaches has increased as a result of increased complexity, uncertainty and interdependence, both approaches face significant challenges in dealing with greater strategic uncertainty. While the strategic direction of the firm is a continuous topic of discussion, decentralised actions are taken to adjust to changing conditions in the case of adaptive approaches or to co-create and change the bigger systems the organisation is part of in the case of transformative approaches to strategy.

What Wiltbank et al. (2006) denote as planning is part of a broader category of prescriptive, rational approaches in strategic management. The earliest contributions in strategic management by and large belong to this stream. Approaches in this category look for the best fit between external opportunities and threats, on the one hand, and distinctive organisational capabilities, on the other, in order to maximise corporate profit-making (Selznick, 1957; Ansoff, 1965; Steiner, 1969; Andrews, 1971). The main responsibility for strategy making lies with the Chief Executive Officer (CEO), who first formulates a full-blown strategy and then sends it to the rest of the organisation for implementation. Rational approaches to strategy making in essence assume that the future context is stable, fully knowable and understandable through analysis and hence predictable. Although approaches differ in the extent to which the strategy process is formalised, the result always is a purposeful, deliberate and explicit strategy translated into a clear set of objectives. Some approaches attach great value to creativity in crafting a unique strategy (e.g. Selznick, 1957); others see a central role for analysis in understanding markets and industries in order to select and secure a competitive market position (e.g. Henderson, 1979; Porter, 1980, 1985, 1996), put strong emphasis on programming the implementation of a selected strategy (e.g. Ansoff, 1965; Kaplan and Norton, 2004) or point to the importance of strategic control to keep strategy on the right track (e.g. Goold and Campbell, 1987; Goold, Campbell and Alexander, 1994). According to Whittington, Cailluet and Yakis-Douglas (2011), rational strategic planning approaches are still widely used by companies and are a core practice of the large strategy-consulting firms.

Contrary to rational planning, the second category of adaptive strategy approaches assumes that the external context is inherently uncertain, complex and volatile. Unexpected emerging events may suddenly shake up the world and innovative technologies can disrupt markets and industries in a short period of time, while new societal demands and changing stakeholder coalitions introduce novel requirements. As a result, cause–effect relationships are unknown, and future conditions are uncertain and cannot be perfectly predicted and planned for in advance. Instead, organisations 'muddle through', avoiding detrimental situations, and learn incrementally through experimentation in order to discover 'satisficing' courses of action (Lindblom, 1959; Quinn, 1980). According to proponents of adaptive strategy approaches, this reflects much more closely how strategies are actually formed in organisations than the idealised rational planning approaches assume. The rituals of planning may even hinder strategic thinking and create blind spots (Mintzberg, 1994). As markets and industries evolve over time and new dynamics, technologies and paradigms present themselves, companies have to master new sets of routines to survive and be successful (Nelson and Winter, 1982; Aldrich and Ruef, 2006; Dahlmann and Brammer, 2011). Moreover, responding adequately and coherently is shaped and challenged by the internal complexities of organisations. Cognitive biases and bounded rationality constrain human thinking and hinder the full selection and processing of relevant information (Cyert and March, 1963), and internal politics and bargaining between coalitions with different interests complicate decision-making (Pettigrew, 1985), while the intricate cultural web that spans the organisation guides collective human action (Johnson, 1987). Organisations that succeed in surviving changing conditions excel in strategic learning and master dynamic capabilities of sensing weak signals of change, seizing the opportunities they bring and changing their organisation when necessary to realise sustainable performance (Thomas, Watts Sussman and Henderson, 2001; Teece, 2007). In the midst of external and internal complexities, strategy reveals itself over time as 'a pattern in a stream of decisions' resulting from deliberate strategy and unintentional, emergent strategy (Mintzberg, 1978: 935; Mintzberg and Waters, 1985).

Rational and adaptive approaches to strategy making see the context in which organisations operate as exogenous and basically out of their control. Identifying the best position or adapting to changing circumstances require either thorough analysis or high organisational agility. Wiltbank et al. (2006) argue that the predictability of future conditions cannot be taken as a necessary condition for the ability to shape and co-create the outside context. To some extent, the latter can be seen as independent from the former. Visionary leaders, for example, assume that the environment is relatively predictable and can be shaped at the same time to achieve desired outcomes. This is an especially powerful perspective to explain and understand the success of disruptive innovators who create entirely new products, services, markets and ecosystems. They foresee or imagine the potential of new technologies and business models and envision how they can contribute or take advantage of it. Examples include successful entrepreneurs from Thomas Edison and Henry Ford to Steve Jobs, Mark Zuckerberg and Elon Musk. Visionary approaches see strategy making largely as informal and 'semi conscious at best', taking place in the mind of a single leader (Mintzberg et al., 2009). Hamel and Prahalad (1989: 65) speak of 'strategic intent', which 'envisions a desired leadership position', 'is more than simply unfettered ambition' and 'encompasses an active management process'. Collins and Porras (1994) argue that the greatest contribution of visionary leaders is not in winning products or services but in the companies they create and build. According to Schilling (2018), three main cognitive processes underlie the creation of visionary strategy: abstract conceptualisation of their market, unconstrained idealism providing long-term focus and long paths of analytical reasoning to craft strategies that are hard to imitate. Using a formal economic model of strategy, Van den Steen (2018) shows that the vision of a CEO can improve strategy execution as long as it concerns decisions over which the CEO has control and which are in line with strong beliefs at the core of the vision about the right course of action. When conditions change often and rapidly, making the future largely unknowable, strong and detailed visions narrow perspectives and can quickly become obsolete (Mintzberg et al., 2009).

The fourth and final category distinguished by Wiltbank et al. (2006) belongs to transformative strategy approaches. These approaches assume that the future business environment is highly uncertain, complex and, as a result, largely unknowable. However, despite the complexity and uncertainty, the environment is not completely uncontrollable. Instead of analysing their context, self-knowledge of available strengths and competences is much more important. Rather than starting from a preconceived vision, transformative strategy approaches see successful organisations maintaining control through discovering opportunities by doing, acting and engaging with others to join available forces and resources and co-create new domains. Wiltbank et al. (2006) put Sarasvathy's (2001) effectuation theory at the heart of this category. Effectuation theory is means-driven rather than goal-oriented and regards entrepreneurship and novel strategies as the outcome of human imagination, which in turn springs from and is reinforced by human aspiration. Change and surprise are opportunities to generate learning such that successes are accumulated and failures outlived (Dew et al., 2008). The focus is on design and co-creation by a coalition of the willing, resulting in entrepreneurial innovation and disruptive transformation in situations of fundamental uncertainty. Transformative approaches to strategy making do not see organisations as existing apart from their environment; both are enacted through social construction and are as such endogenous to each other (Smircich and Stubbart, 1985). Strategy formation is a highly interactive, interpretive, creative and symbolic activity aimed at creating and maintaining shared meaning that initiates collective action. In this view, contextual analysis in itself is superfluous, but it can play a role in challenging current perspectives and creating multiple interpretations of what is going on in order to inform new actions. Rather than adapting to an external environment, organisations actively shape their future contexts, including imagined, idealised ecosystems (Patvardhan and Ramachandran, 2020).

3.3 Strategy-as-Practice

In addition to existing approaches and perspectives on strategy making, Whittington (1996) points to the, by then emerging, perspective of strategy as 'practice'. Ever since, research on the praxis and practices of strategy has been expanding rapidly (Johnson, Melin and Whittington,2003; Rouleau, 2013). Strategy-as-practice highlights the social dimension of strategy and focuses on what strategy practitioners actually do, as well as what it takes to be effective as a practitioner. It builds on many of the insights generated by approaches that focus on organisational processes of strategy making from an adaptive perspective in particular but seeks to draw attention to the individual managerial level. By doing so, strategy-as-practice brings human actors and their actions into the area of strategy, which was absent in most abstract strategy theories (Jarzabkowski and Spee, 2009). Given the increasing fluidity of resources and the speed, surprise and innovation of hypercompetitive markets, strategy making has become a continuous process and, as such, requires an activity-based view on strategy to gain insight into complexities of managerial and organisational action (Johnson, Melin and Whittington, 2003). In fact, strategising and organising are so 'similar and intermingled in action that it is hardly worth trying to tell them apart' (Whittington et al., 2006: 618).

From the perspective of strategy-as-practice, strategy is not so much what an organisation 'has' as it is broadly conceptualised as a situated, socially accomplished activity of how strategy practitioners act, interact and negotiate with their wider social group and the symbolic artefacts that are involved (Jarzabkowski, Balogun and Seidl, 2007; Jarzabkowski and Spee, 2009). This includes all concrete activities performed, the knowledge, tools and skills drawn upon, the routines consciously and unconsciously applied, the different roles played and the workshops, conversations and discourses practitioners contribute to (Rouleau, 2013). Strategy-as-practice explicitly acknowledges the role of hands-on, practical crafting skills in strategy making as introduced by Mintzberg (1987). However, instead of doubting the effectiveness of strategy-planning approaches altogether, Whittington et al. (2006) call for applying the craft metaphor to deliberate strategy making too, with the aim of making it more informal, creative and dynamic.

Strategy practitioners include everyone directly involved in making strategy and those who exert their influence indirectly (Jarzabkowski and Whittington, 2008). Prominent among the first group are top executives, general managers, senior staffers, board members and hired consultants. To those with indirect influence belong all those an organisation has direct relations with, such as stakeholders, alliance partners, customers and suppliers but also 'the policymakers, the media, reputational agents, the gurus and the business schools who shape legitimate praxis and practices' (Jarzabkowski and Whittington, 2008: 101–2). The practice of strategy differs across the various kinds of strategy practitioners, each with a distinct mix of activities and competences, depending on their position, role and activities in strategy making. In line with this, effective practitioners know how to perform their role in getting things done within a particular context and culture: 'the craft skills of strategizing are not general and success in one role is no guarantee of success in another' (Whittington, 1996: 732). The creation of strategy may be different at the periphery and in the centre of organisations, as Regnér (2003) observes, with the former being more inductive and exploratory and the latter more deductive and formal. This suggests that the practice of strategy may vary across different approaches to strategy making.

In planning approaches, effective strategy practices include analysing market dynamics, running workshops to bring insights together, deducing the perfect match with organisational resources, formulating and communicating full-blown strategies, creating a coherent set of objectives and steering and monitoring strategy implementation. As adaptive approaches see the environment as inherently uncertain and dynamic, effective strategy practitioners excel in detecting weak signals of emerging change and immediately adjusting corporate strategy and organisation adequately and coherently while learning on the way and skillfully riding the waves of organisational culture and politics. In visionary approaches, organisational leaders are the dominant strategy practitioners who succeed as no other in getting the unanimous support of a diverse group of actors in building the company that is required to realise the idealised long-term future they have in mind. Finally, in transformative strategy approaches, strategy emerges on the way as strategy practitioners master the skills to probe and experiment with others and continuously co-create and change supportive business networks. Overall, given the complementarity of strategy approaches, effective strategy practitioners are able to select the appropriate approach given their assessment of environmental uncertainty and control. To be successful in the long term, it is essential to manage ambidextrous requirements related to simultaneously pursuing evolutionary and revolutionary change (Tushman and O'Reilly, 1996; Regnér, 2003).

Given growing complexity and uncertainty, board members need to develop and master strategy practices in line with more adaptive and transformative approaches to strategy making. Practices need to contribute to the dynamic capabilities that are, according to Teece (2007), essential to operate, cooperate and innovate in emerging business environments. This framework aims to understand how firms can create value when uncertainty is ubiquitous (Teece,

Peteraf and Leih 2016). When the complexity and uncertainty of business environments is considered high, quickly testing underlying strategy and business model assumptions is preferred to planning far ahead. Sustainable corporate performance is then largely driven by trial-and-error rather than ex ante foresight. Transition paths emerge in ongoing interaction with the environment and hence require a transformative approach to strategy making. To manage in environments surrounded by high complexity and uncertainty requires probing, experimenting and generating and testing of multiple hypotheses.

3.4 Purpose as Strategy

In the foregoing, we have pointed to the growing volatility, ambiguity, complexity and uncertainty that firms face and have to cope with. Social change, rapid technological innovation and disruptive business models can shake up markets and industries in short periods of time. The simultaneous exploitation of current activities in the shorter term to generate sufficient resources to invest in the exploration and building of new value-creating avenues in the longer term are often at odds with each other in terms of organisational learning and management logics (March, 1991). Pursuing both evolutionary and revolutionary change confronts firms with the innovator's dilemma and requires ambidextrous organising and leadership, which have proven to be extremely challenging in practice and demand well-coordinated processes (Tushman and O'Reilly, 1996; Christensen, 1997; Raisch and Tushman, 2016). Also, the boundaries of the firm are increasingly fading as business activities become intricately connected in integrated systems. Exploring new frontiers asks for close cooperation among a broad variety of partners in and across business networks and innovative ecosystems (Adner and Kapoor, 2010; Autio and Thomas, 2014), and the more so in the context of inevitable secondary and behavioural uncertainty (Koopmans, 1957; Helfat and Teece, 1987; Williamson, 1985). The continuing shift towards intangible assets, tacit competences and mutual firm-specific investments makes this joint value creation even more challenging (Mayer, Wright and Phan, 2017).

Meanwhile, firms are under growing pressure to pay more attention to value creation in the longer term, as well as to contribute to the well-being of society and the inherent transformation that it demands. A widening group of stakeholders, as well as the general public, increasingly holds boards responsible for contributing to a broad array of social, economic and environmental concerns and challenges, as summarised in general terms in the '17 United Nations Sustainable Development Goals' (United Nations, 2015). As the concept of economic rent stretches to a broader notion of social value creation, multiple stakeholders join shareholders with residual claims on the value created by a firm and the broader business networks they are part of. The purpose of the firm broadens from creating value for shareholders towards contributing to sustainable societies and ecologies in a profitable way. In line with this, the orientation of firms continues to shift from the shorter towards to the longer term. As a result, a focus on current shareholders and other stakeholders is too narrow, as their interests may not necessarily align with long-term value creation for the broader benefit of society. Instead, the purpose of a firm is derived from contributing to higher-level societal challenges, and hence the focus of the board shifts to the firm's contribution to those. Being part of society rather than apart from society, the core purpose of the firm is to positively transform and contribute to the well-being of the broader society, of which shareholders and stakeholders are only selective groups (Hollensbe et al., 2014). In fact, the purpose signifies the reason for existence of the firm and informs strategy making and strategic choices made by the firm (Younger, Mayer and Eccles, 2020).

Growing environmental uncertainty, collaboration in broader business networks and the shift towards wider societal transformation change the nature of value creation in terms of strategic portfolio, process and routines, and performance metrics. In environments that are constantly changing and in which novel systems emerge in co-creation, both classic strategic planning and adaptive approaches that merely adapt to changing circumstances do not suffice, while visionary approaches may lead into and follow dead-end roads or do not contribute to societal purpose. As unknown and unpredictable futures unfold, transformative approaches to strategy making are required to create value in the longer term. Given the intricate connectedness of value-creating systems and higher-level purpose, intensive collaboration between a diverse set of actors and stakeholders within innovative business networks and ecosystems stands at the core of this. Whereas transformative approaches by themselves create high strategic uncertainty for stakeholders, probing and experimenting with others in and outside firm boundaries in broader and often ill-defined business networks increases uncertainty even further. This creates coordination problems that cannot be handled through vertical integration, the most preferred twentieth-century firm response in static business environments. In twenty-first-century dynamics, desired outcomes are by and large unknown, and strategic visions, required competences and suitable partners vary over time depending on continuously changing conditions and demands. Instead of reducing strategic uncertainty through corporate integration, planning and incentives, embracing uncertainty through alignment in broader business networks has to take place in other ways.

As the purpose of the firm broadens from contributing to shareholders and stakeholders to serving the well-being of society in close cooperation with a variety of partners and institutions, interrelated activities have to be aligned across all actors to the societal purpose to which they together contribute. The long-term value creation of the individual firm and its strategy then corresponds with the broader societal purpose and is hence directly derived from this purpose (Younger, Mayer and Eccles, 2020). As an additional advantage, this alignment increases trust in the firm in general and between the actors collaborating in business networks in particular. There are two specific mechanisms to create, maintain and, when required, dynamically change alignment to purpose over time. The first is through sharing and keeping alive the core values that are at the heart of it. In the context of a single firm, Hollensbe et al. (2014) discuss several values that are directly related to the defined purpose and, in doing so, inspire their employees: human dignity, solidarity with others, valuing plurality, responsibility based on subsidiarity, reciprocity of mutual benefit and environmental sustainability. In a similar way, this purpose as culture may act as a mechanism to align activities across business networks, while inspiring current contributors and attracting others. In doing so, shared values reinforce the corporate purpose, trust, interrelations and stewardship within and across collaborating firms.

The second way to align the purpose of a firm with the business networks and ecosystems it collaborates in and the societal challenge it contributes to is through collective strategy making, i.e. purpose as strategy. When future conditions are uncertain and transformative strategy approaches are the preferred mode, this requires an ongoing strategic conversation between all those that are directly and indirectly involved. In the context of open innovation, Chesbrough and Appleyard (2006) introduce the concept of open strategy as a way to coordinate invention efforts across business networks and grow a new user base. They note that existing strategy approaches primarily focus on asset ownership to achieve market success and underestimate, or even fully ignore, the role and benefits of external resources firms share with others. The importance of resources such as crowdsourcing, voluntary contributions and innovative ecosystems have grown sharply over time. Rather than concentrating on defending established market positions and raising barriers to entry, many growing companies instead invest in the expansion of open initiatives as a basis to build and extend their activities. Whittington, Cailluet and Yakis-Douglas (2011) observe that developments such as the blurring of organisational boundaries, growing managerial mobility, popularisation of strategy, information-sharing technologies and pressure from external stakeholders foster further openness of strategy making, both in terms of inclusion of groups of stakeholders and transparent sharing of information. Appleyard and Chesbrough (2017) note that choosing open strategy making is not a once-and-for-all decision. They argue that it may be more beneficial when developing new technologies and building a customer base and less so when a firm has accumulated enough superior technology prowess and does not need the broader community any more.

Like former approaches to strategy, open strategy by and large starts from the perspective and interest of a single firm. Birkinshaw (2017) distinguishes between four aspects of the open strategy phenomenon: commons-based peer production, crowd-based input when formulating strategies, collective buy-in and action to enable smooth implementation and collective sense-making of a firm's chosen strategy in the capital market. Of these four, only the first goes partially beyond the scope and purpose of a single actor. According to Benkler and Nissenbaum (2006: 394), participants in commons-based peer production cooperate to create 'information, knowledge or cultural goods without relying on either market pricing or managerial hierarchies to coordinate their common enterprise'. They note that the virtues that these collaborations foster are partly self-regarding and partly social in nature. The latter can be given to others who need and benefit from it or to a commons, community or mission of which the contributor is a member. In the latter case, the members cooperate to create and maintain something of value for all or to a greater purpose beyond the collective itself.

4 Strategy and Purpose and the Role of the Board

4.1 Models of Corporate Governance

As indicated in the Introduction, corporate governance concerns institutions that create and allocate power and influence over decision-making about control and direction of the corporation. In this respect, Adam Smith wrote in the *Wealth of Nations*:

> The trade of a joint stock company is always managed by a court of directors. This court, indeed, is frequently subject, in many respects, to the control of a general court of proprietors. But the greater part of those proprietors seldom pretend to understand anything of the business of the company; and when the spirit of faction happens not to prevail among them, give themselves no trouble about it, but receive contentedly such half- or yearly dividend, as the directors think proper to make them . . . The directors of such companies, however, being the managers of other people's money than of their own, it cannot be well expected that they should watch over it with the same anxious vigilance with which the partners in a private copartnery frequently watch

over their own ... Negligence and profusion, therefore, must always prevail, more or less, in the management of the affairs of such a company. (Smith, 1776: 699–700)

The quote may be taken as a first illustration of the separation of ownership and control and one of the first descriptions of what still largely is considered the basic problem of corporate governance: the asymmetry of information between knowledgeable directors and non-competent proprietors. More generally, the broad characteristics of the relationships between the different constituents of the corporation have served as the most relevant components of alternative models and theories of corporate governance in the extant literature. In this section, we make an attempt to characterise those models, building upon the extant literature, in order to arrive at defining alternatives that can be distinguished by their relationship characteristics and governance objectives. After having identified the alternative corporate-governance models, we will in subsequent sections zoom in on the roles and objectives of the most relevant component of internal governance, the board of directors.

Most directly related to the ancient conceptualisation of Adam Smith is *principal–agent theory*, which approaches corporate governance from the perspective of the relationship between the shareholders of the corporation and the managers. The principal–agent theory presumes rational self-interest of actors. Within corporate governance, this implies that more knowledgeable managers, acting as agents on behalf of the owners as principals, choose to maximise their own utility. Thus the corporate governance problem arises in the case where management interests are not aligned with shareholder interests (Jensen and Meckling, 1976). To mitigate costs resulting from principal–agent conflicts, *principal–agent theory* introduces incentive alignment through performance contracts in combination with close monitoring of managers to resolve the gaps left in the incomplete performance contracts. The board is introduced as an internal governance mechanism to administer incentive contracts and monitoring activities. In a similar approach to human decision-making, but focusing on the problem of free-riding within productive teams, *team production theory* builds on the conception that companies are bundles of assets where a productive activity by the corporate team requires the combined investment and coordinated effort of two or more individuals or groups (Blair, 2004). Given incomplete contracts, preventing free-riding behaviour requires an internal hierarchy as a second-best solution in order to coordinate the activity of team members and to prevent them pursuing their own interests (Blair and Stout, 1999). Compared to principal–agent theory, *stakeholder theory* takes the interest of multiple stakeholders into account in the governance of firms (Freeman, 1984). Corporations are considered multilateral agreements among stakeholders and institutional arrangements for governing relationships between all of the parties that contribute any firm-specific assets. This theory weighs the interests of all stakeholders and holds that the top management and the board manage and balance the diversity of interests and establish and maintain relationships with the main stakeholders. In doing so, the legitimacy of the organisation in the external environment is also fostered. Harrison and St John (1996) suggest that external stakeholder relationships can be managed, contingent on the strategic importance of these stakeholders. An alternative to agency theory and stakeholder theory that gained ground and is helpful in understanding the relationship between principals and managers is *stewardship theory* (see Donaldson and Davis, 1991). Instead of assuming opportunistic and self-serving actors, stewardship theory regards managers as reliable, supportive stewards, who identify themselves with the best interest of the entire corporation and focus on common responsibilities, intrinsic satisfaction, cooperation and altruism (Arthurs and Busenitz, 2003; Donaldson and Davis, 1991). Stewardship theory builds on cooperative behaviour in the relationship between managers and principals (Davis, Schoorman and Donaldson, 1997). The cooperative relationship between principals, directors and managers and other stakeholders is seen as developing from trust, intrinsic motivation, sharing information and dialogue. In this view, directors support managers through providing expert services. Informal, more equivalent governance relationships gain relevance, and in particular, the trust relationships among directors and between directors and managers and their principals are a central element of stewardship theory (Donaldson and Davis, 1991).

Building upon the aforementioned theories and by taking a holistic perspective, alternative corporate-governance configurations or models can be developed. In the shareholder primacy model, maximising shareholder value is the ultimate purpose of the firm. In the stakeholder governance view, this view is stretched to value creation with and for a broader set of constituencies, in order to meet respective interests. Finally, in purpose governance the articulation of the purpose of the firm in society reflects a process of continuous strategic change. In *shareholder governance*, shareholders are the principal stakeholders. Incentive contracts and efficient joint production serve to involve other stakeholders. The board functions as the formal strategic apex of the organisation and is as their trustee accountable to ensure value for shareholders. Much of the mainstream literature on corporate governance has concentrated on shareholder primacy, principal–agent problems and the collective-action problem among dispersed investors (cf. Becht, Bolton and Roëll, 2002). The reconciliation of conflicts of interest between managers and investors and among corporate claimholders are the central elements in this literature, where the focus is prescriptive and concentrates on compliance and accountability (see Ingley and Van der Walt, 2001). Accountability to shareholders and control of management and the CEO is the main focus. By contrast, in *stakeholder governance*, stakeholders collaborate on a more equal footing to create value in order to realise their possibly opposing stakeholder interests. Contracting and control serve to connect and respond to internal and external stakeholders, while striving for efficiency and consulting the stakeholders during production. Lastly, in *purpose governance*, the common articulation and realisation of the corporate purpose is the key element; stakeholders are considered intrinsically motivated, supporting the realisation of the corporate purpose as stewards. The corporate contribution to society is its reason for existence, and enacting purpose and engaging stakeholders through communicating purpose is the central strategic focus. Directors focus on enacting purpose through co-articulation of the purpose and the strategy to realise that purpose and are as such responsive to society. In purpose-driven production, internal and external networks of stakeholders collaborate through the focal organisation's purpose articulation and its strategy to realise that purpose. The commitment of stakeholders is essential for joint value creation, and hence the attention of the board for their perspectives and motivations to join the corporation. Thus to conclude, alternative corporate governance configurations can be distinguished that differ for instance in their orientation towards stakeholders, value creation and protection, the embedded idea of justice, stakeholder motivation and engagement, the primacy of efficiency and effectiveness and the style of governance (authoritative, consultative or deliberative. a) Table 2 summarises the main elements of each governance configuration.

Note that the aforementioned corporate governance models reflect ideal types and that interesting combinations may be developed. For instance, by combining elements of stakeholder and more purpose-driven governance, Bridoux and Stoelhorst (2014) develop two alternative approaches to stakeholder relationships for sustained value creation, the fairness approach and an arms-length approach. Two mechanisms impact value creation by stakeholders: (1) a motivational effect that recognises that stakeholders can be categorised into self-regarding and reciprocal contributors, caring about personal pay-offs or with an inclination to reward fair and punish unfair treatment of self and others, respectively; and (2) a sorting effect over time that determines which stakeholders will join, stay or leave the firm. They subsequently explain that a fairness approach may be more effective in attracting, retaining and motivating reciprocal stakeholders to create value, and an arms-length approach is more effective in attracting, retaining and motivating self-regarding stakeholders

Table 2 Alternative corporate governance models

	Shareholder governance	Stakeholder governance	Purpose governance
Alignment	Incentive contract / control	Incentive contract / control	Corporate purpose
View on organisation	Governance mechanism to serve shareholder needs	Governance mechanism to serve stakeholder needs	Governance mechanism to serve societal needs
Motivation	Extrinsic and self-regarding	Extrinsic and reciprocal	Intrinsic and reciprocal
Company focus	Shareholder value	Stakeholder value	Societal impact
Governance focus	Value distribution	Value distribution	Value creation and configuration
Concept of justice	Distributive	Distributive	Contributive
Value concept	Profit maximisation	Stakeholder benefits	Contribution to society
View of voluntariness	Contract	Contract	Stewardship and commitment
Governance process focus	Efficiency	Efficiency	Effectiveness
Governance style	Authoritative / show	Consultative	Inclusive / deliberative
Governance orientation	Shareholder interest	Stakeholder interest	Collective well-being
Accountability	Accountability to shareholders	Accountability to stakeholders	Accountability to society

with high bargaining power. For stakeholder management, the authors develop the categorisation depicted in Table 3 (Bridoux and Stoelhorst, 2014: 107–10).

To some extent, these approaches resemble leadership styles, such as transactional leadership and transformational leadership (see Table 4). While transactional leadership uses management by exception and monitors deviations from rules and standards, intervening only when standards are not met, avoids making decisions, rewards good performance and contracts the exchange of rewards for effort, transformational leadership provides vision, instills pride, gains respect and trust, communicates high expectations, expresses important

Table 3 Alternative approaches to stakeholders

Practices with respect to	Arms-length	Fairness
Value capture	Bargaining power drives value appropriation among stakeholders	Fairness drives value distribution among stakeholders
Information exchange	Secrecy and information asymmetry	Open, transparent collaboration
Contracts	Elaborate formal contracts, monitoring and incentives, short-term relationships among stakeholders	Not detailed, trust and self-enforcement, long-lasting relationships among stakeholders

Table 4 Alternative leadership styles

Leadership style	Transactional	Transformative
Decision makers	Opportunistic and self-regarding	Shared interest / reciprocal
Nature of the firm	Nexus of contracts	Nexus of relationships
Attitude of stakeholders	Self-interest	Stewardship and trust
Transactions	At arms length, governed through incentive contracts	Relational via shared purpose and commitment
Motivation	Extrinsic	Intrinsic

purposes in simple ways, promotes intelligence, rationality, and careful problem solving, gives personal attention, coaches and advises (see Gordon, 1993: 352).

4.2 The Board of Directors

The board of directors is seen as the most relevant component of internal corporate governance. Director activities can be divided into executive and non-executive tasks. Tasks can be formally combined into a unitary or one-tier board structure or formally separated in a two-tier structure. The nature of board tasks is cognitive and constitutes obtaining, sharing and processing information (see Rindova, 1999; Forbes and Milliken, 1999). The complexity of board tasks increases with uncertainty and complexity of the environment. Board activities aim at creating accountability, responsiveness, legitimacy, transparency, continuity and engagement. The effectiveness of the board as part of corporate governance can thus be defined as the realisation of the aforementioned objectives through board activities related to corporate purpose and strategy. Table 5 defines the board objectives in more detail.

Directors have the fiduciary duty from all internal and external stakeholders to exercise decision rights and can be held accountable and responsible to the stakeholders, depending on governance configurations.The firm's long-term continuity is dependent on the capacity to secure resources (tangible and intangible, for exploiting existing business models and exploring new ones) and the preservation of legitimacy and transparency towards the stakeholders while investing these specific assets. Traditionally, the focus of the board is to monitor performance and risks and sometimes to act as strategic advisor (cf. Tricker, 1994). From this perspective, the board's primary role as the decision-making apex is to act in the best interest of the shareholders, as residual claimants. With the number of a firm's strategic stakeholders increasing, the board's *responsibility* and *accountability* to shareholders is shifting to *responsiveness* to all stakeholders and to society at large (e.g. Tirole, 2001). An alternative perspective perceives that the board's main task is to focus on value creation, rather than value distribution among stakeholders (Huse, 2007, 2009). Finally, to the extent that businesses give way to serving their corporate purpose over profits, it becomes more critical for the board to align stakeholders around the stated purpose. The nature of board objectives and the focus of board activities can be seen as contextualised within alternative corporate governance configurations as outlined in the previous section. Table 6 positions board objectives and activities in alternative corporate governance configurations.

Also, the aforementioned corporate governance theories can be connected to the functioning of the board in alternative corporate governance configurations.

Table 5 Board objectives and effectiveness

	Board effectiveness = the realisation of board objectives				
Board objective	Creating continuity = continuity of corporate operations and the corporate entity	Creating accountability = to explicate the reasons for undertaking corporate activities and to provide the normative grounds for which these may be justified	Creating engagement = the formal or informal willingness to contribute to or collaborate in realising corporate purpose	Creating legitimacy = creating popular acceptance of corporate activities and the implications of these activities	Creating transparency = making corporate activities and their implications observable by outsiders

Table 6 Board activities is alternative corporate governance configurations

		Governance configuration		
Board objective		**Shareholder governance**	**Stakeholder governance**	**Purpose governance**
	Creating accountability	Accountability to financial investors	Accountability to stakeholder coalitions	Accountability of realisation of purpose to society
	Creating legitimacy	Legitimacy primarily to financial investors and regulators	Legitimacy to dominant stakeholder coalitions and regulators	Legitimacy to stakeholders and wider society
	Creating transparency	Transparency to financial investors and regulators	Transparency to dominant coalitions and regulators	Transparency to all stakeholders and society at large
	Creating engagement	Long-term engagement of financial investors (shareholders)	Long-term engagement of strategic stakeholders	Long-term engagement with corporate purpose of strategic stakeholders
	Assuring continuity	Assuring sound financial risk / return combinations	Assuring sound risk / stakeholder return combinations	Assuring impact under the condition of affordable loss

Shareholder governance builds upon principal–agent theory and primarily focuses on the board's role of monitoring and controlling management. Stakeholder governance rests upon stakeholder theory and accounts for the alignment of interests among a firm's internal and external stakeholders. Incorporating stakeholder interest helps to strengthen the links between the organisation and the external environment (Williamson, 1996) and to secure critical resources (Pfeffer and Salancik, 1978). Co-opting independent non-executive directors onto the board as representatives of employees or governments is, for example, particularly prevalent in continental-European countries, such as Germany, Sweden and the Netherlands. Stakeholder alignment may also create legitimacy. The role of the boards here is to support management through their capacity to connect to strategic stakeholders and other important outside resources. In purpose governance, stewardship theory is most prevalent. The board's role is primarily supplying their directors' competences (e.g. experience, knowledge and counselling) and aligning interests of stakeholders. By fostering trust, information exchange and dialogue, the board is supportive in forging good relationships and cohesion between strategic internal and external stakcholders, so that all constituents are committed to act as stewards for the corporation (e.g. Kaufman and Englander, 2011) and when needed to mitigate the risk of free-riding (Blair and Stout, 1999).

4.3 Board Roles

Following Mace's (1971) seminal publication on the roles of the corporate board, the extant literature has gone to great length to further specify and detail a wide range of alternative board roles. Next to monitoring, Johnson, Daily and Ellstrand (1996) distinguish the roles of advice and strategic participation to support management and engagement in the process of strategy making (see also, e.g., Zahra and Pearce, 1989; McNulty and Pettigrew, 1999; Ravasi and Zattoni, 2006). In line with resource dependency theory's focus on securing a stable flow of resources, boards can play a role in reducing uncertainty, acquiring resources and diffusing information by creating multiple connections between the organisation and its environment (e.g. Pfeffer and Salancik, 1978). From a holistic perspective, these roles define the board as a (pro)active strategic decision-making group (Forbes and Milliken, 1999; Pugliese et al., 2009; Rindova, 1999). To characterise the board's engagement, Kendry and Kiel (2004) differentiate between a passive and an active role for boards, which corresponds with Useem's (2012) shareholder monitoring and strategic partnering as main strategic role-functions of the board. The shareholder monitoring model prescribes that directors oversee the management of the firm's strategic practices and serve as vigilant monitors of the strategies on behalf of shareholders. Strategic partnering expects directors to fulfil their role as strategic partners of managers, engaging in strategic decisions. In order to prevent passivity, corporate governance codes and legislation, introduction programmes and courses have been developed to shape the behaviour of directors and improve their functioning as involved professionals. Active or engaged partnering boards take responsibility for establishing and shaping objectives, enabling broad and general policy decisions by managers, and fuel a continuous dialogue with internal and external stakeholders on how to realise the corporate purpose. In this respect, rather than remaining at a distance, developing a trust-based relationship between the board of directors and top management may be essential. Thus instead of identifying detailed but separate board roles, board behaviour may be better conceptualised as a continuum of interacting activities of approving, monitoring and reviewing strategy, providing leadership and active engagement with defining and establishing purpose and values and setting direction (see Ingley and Van der Walt, 2001; Sundaramurthy and Lewis, 2003). The primary focus of the board is in the strategy process from initiation to implementation and in evaluating strategy in light of the corporate purpose (cf. McNulty and Pettigrew, 1999; McKinsey, 2016). The board's role in overseeing and advising top management and consequently also its role in strategy implies the involvement of the board in all aspects of strategy making. In particular, McNulty and Pettigrew (1999) indicate that contributing to strategy making is the core role of the board, which all activities are part of, directly and indirectly contribute to and are hence derived from. Put differently, all activities that are performed by board members, whether monitoring, strategy and service or networking, are an integral and interdependent part of their contribution to strategy, and a conceptual separation in distinct categories neglects the interdependency and can be regarded as a redundant exercise in abstract theorising.

Focusing on strategy, McNulty and Pettigrew (1999) observe that non-executive board members perform three distinct but complementary kinds of strategic roles in interaction with top management: taking strategic decisions, shaping strategic decisions and shaping the content, context and conduct of strategic decisions. In the case of taking strategic decisions, the board exerts influence at the end of the capital-investment decision process as prepared by top management. When board members shape strategic decisions, their influence starts early in the strategic decision process, as they also shape the preparation of strategic decisions and capital-investment proposals by executives. In its most extensive role, the board's influence is continuous and not limited to distinct episodes of strategy making. The board sets the context for strategic dialogue, establishes the methodology for strategy development and stimulates executives to think strategically. It can furthermore be added that these stereotypical modes of board involvement represent three stages of increasing influence and activity, ranging from the end of the strategic decision-making process, before and during the proposal development stage to continuous and ongoing involvement. Based on their research, McNulty and Pettigrew (1999) conclude that all boards take strategic decisions, some also shape strategic decisions and only a minority shape the context, content and conduct of strategy. More specifically, they found that with rejection rates between 5 and 10 per cent (the highest rate quoted was only 20 per cent), boards approve by far the majority of proposals put forward by executives, which suggests that the majority of boards adopt a 'rubber-stamping' mode.

McNulty and Pettigrew (1999) also explore the conditions that encourage board members to expand their role in strategy making. These include a more prominent role in corporate governance, performance weaknesses, corporate scandals and increased shareholder activism, all of which have increased considerably in the past two decades. Related to corporate strategy itself, they note that the involvement of board members grows in cases of international expansion, acquisitions, mergers and divestitures. They also note that the way in which boards function internally also determines how actively they are involved in strategy making. When strategy is the most relevant item on the board's agenda, formal and informal processes of information-sharing, challenge and debate and allotted strategy days increase active involvement of the board. Boards that allow 'shades of opinion' within executive teams 'have a greater flow of information and wider perspective against which they can probe and question strategy' (McNulty and Pettigrew, 1999: 69).

Since the seminal publication of McNulty and Pettigrew (1999), research has studied both the characteristics of boards that engage more in strategy making, the roles they adopt and the impact they have. Some studies conclude, in line with McNulty and Pettigrew's (1999) findings, that the role of the board in strategy making is by and large passive; others note that boards take on a more active role depending on board characteristics and strategic context. Using a multimethod approach to examine the impact of boards on strategy in UK public companies, Stiles (2001: 646) concludes that 'although boards limit their role on coordinating and checking consistency and coherence among proposed strategies' by business units and division, in performing this role 'minimal activity seems to be rare'. In a study of boards in large

Italian firms, Pugliese, Minichilli and Zattoni (2014) found that boards engage less in both monitoring and advice tasks when the company is performing well, whereas more industry regulation enhances both tasks. In a study in the US hospital industry, Golden and Zajac (2001) found that, especially for more powerful boards, board characteristics such as size, tenure and heterogeneity have, up to a certain level, a positive effect on their role in strategic change. In addition, board members from a business context are more open to strategic change, while organisations with more powerful boards, who are more inclined to strategic change, actually succeed better in actually realising change. If and when boards perform their strategy roles also depends on factors internal and external to the firm. Altman and Tushman (2017) argue that boards may play a more active role by providing introductions and network connections during the transition towards emerging business networks, open-user platforms and innovative ecosystems, as these generate more boundary-spanning activities. Based on a study among large stock-listed companies, Haynes and Hillman (2010) conclude that more heterogeneous boards, in terms of human and social capital, bring in more and more diverse network connections, which contributes to more strategic change. Finally, research indicates that active involvement of boards in strategy making in firms induces positive performance effects. In a study among large US companies over a period of nine years, Walls and Hoffman (2013) studied the extent of deviance from institutional norms to enhance environmental sustainability and found strong support that boards with more extensive environmental experience are more likely to deviate positively. Zattoni, Gnan and Huse (2015), in a study among small and medium-sized family enterprises, found that, unlike board control tasks, strategy tasks executed by boards lead to an increase in financial performance.

This concludes our short digression on the extant literature on board roles. In the next section, we will develop the role of the board in more detail by focusing on corporate purpose and strategy, taking the conceptual framework developed in McNulty and Pettigrew (1999) as our reference.

4.4 The Role of the Board in Corporate Purpose and Strategy

4.4.1 Corporate Purpose and the Role the Board

Purpose articulates why an organisation exists. Purpose as strategy provides the board and stakeholders with a shared strategic direction. A clear corporate purpose motivates internal and external corporate constituents to perform better in a changing context, and as such it guides strategic decisions and activities.

Clarity of purpose helps boards to make better-informed decisions to transform their organisation. Values directing how the organisation operates, a mission as to what the organisation does and a vision of how the organisation aspires to make an impact, all are directly derived from the corporate purpose. The board of directors has the primary responsibility of defining the purpose, enacting it through values and mission and connecting it to the organisation's long-term aspiration. Subsequently, the strategy brings the purpose into practice (see Younger, Mayer and Eccles, 2020).

Among others, McNulty, Zattoni and Douglas (2013) and Pugliese, Minichilli and Zattoni (2014) argue that effective boards will be held accountable in relation to a larger and more diverse range of stakeholders. The corporation reflects the nexus of stakeholder relationships with and without a priori assumptions on organisational goals and objectives. This perspective illustrates the importance of the board's role in setting corporate purpose, creating engagement and alignment of goals and objectives as influenced by power plays and politics in and between coalitions of stakeholders, including society at large. Engagement can be defined as a relational process between corporations and stakeholders that develops through different influence processes and intent in an ongoing relationship involving mutual exchanges aimed at understanding (see McNulty and Nordberg, 2016: 346). Boards can foster engagement as a two-way street through communicative dynamics, learning and political dynamics (cf. Gond et al., 2018). For stakeholder engagement to become real, commitment to purpose starts from the top, that is, the board. Boards are responsible to the firm's constituents for the continuity of the company; it is their role to define purpose or to initiate the narrative that underlines the reason for existence, as well as to make sure the corporation will be able to continue activities to enact purpose.

Purpose-driven corporations form to govern stakeholders who voluntarily assemble because they value the purpose realised by the collective in a way that will outpass the aggregate of the individual efforts and resources (Klein et al., 2012, 2019). The corporation does not aim to fulfil the interests of stakeholders but pursues a strategy to realise the shared corporate purpose. Organisations thus thrive as bundles of shared intentions, values and relationships among stakeholders who invest their firm-specific assets into purpose-driven and meaningful activities. The corporate governance problem that arises is how to effectively address three interdependent challenges by agreement: (1) the selection of purpose, (2) an individual responsibility problem concerning the cooperative activities to generate corporate purpose and (3) a collective responsibility problem regarding the enabling of individual needs and preferences in view of the enactment of purpose of the corporation as a whole. This extended objective of corporate governance is to successfully address these challenges in mutual interaction, so as to connect the intentions and capabilities of diverse stakeholders in a way that fosters the realisation of the purpose of the organisation and the continuity and legitimacy of the corporation in the midst of uncertainty and holds the corporation accountable to the wider business environment. When successful, stakeholders serve the corporation as stewards, embodying an ethic of responsible and sustainable governance of corporate and actor-specific intentions and capabilities.

Similarly to the other corporate governance configurations, in purpose governance the role of the board is also to safeguard the continuity of the corporation. The continuity of the corporation is crucially dependent on the commitment of stakeholders and the legitimacy of the corporation within wider society. Hence the role of the board is to guide and guard both legitimacy and stakeholder engagement. Broadly speaking, this role assigns the board authority at the apex of the organisation in strategic processes of sense making and meaning of corporate activities and in guiding and guarding collaborative relationships of stakeholders. This role emphasises the relevance for the organisation of making sense of a complex and uncertain reality in relation to its reason for existence (purpose), of being held accountable for the realisation of purpose and of being able to anticipate and respond to potential changes and surprises, threats and opportunities (alertness) that may affect continuity and stakeholder relationships. The role may include several activities (see also Section 4.5). First and in line with, amongst others, Pugliese, Minichilli and Zattoni (2014), particularly in purpose governance, effective boards create accountability towards a larger and more diverse range of stakeholders, including societal stakeholders. This perspective emphasises the board leadership in deliberative processes that (re)define purpose and related objectives as influenced through interactions with and within and between coalitions of stakeholders, including society at large (see also Section 2). Second, board practice is to develop relational governance modes that match and connect the dispositions of the existing stakeholders in a way that fosters trust and commitment to purpose-driven and sustainable joint value creation. Third, to assure alertness, the board has an important task in critically challenging top executives concerning their implicit underlying assumptions of the strategic intentions and activities of the corporation in relation to the purpose of the corporation. Fourth, the board can be proactive in exploring opportunities and threats next to the ratification of strategic decisions. These activities require a sounding board and a more direct involvement and engagement of the members of the board in strategic decision-making at proximity to executive board members. Such an actionable perspective on board practices implies that effective boards will be engaged in a more extended menu of strategic activities by shaping strategic content and context in a dialogue with top management (see Section 4.4.2 on the board's role in strategy).

To elaborate more on the role of the board in particular in garnering the engagement of stakeholders, much of the literature on value creation assumes conflicts of interest among stakeholders. Thus, assuming fixed resources of material benefits, problems of agency abound, as –almost by definition – satisfying the interests of one implies disregarding the interests of the other. By contrast, Harrison and Wicks (2013) define four dimensions of joint value creation: (1) stakeholder value associated with actual goods and services (economic value); (2) stakeholder value associated with organisational justice (fairness value, reciprocity in dyadic and network relationships and trust); (3) stakeholder value from affiliation (social value, social identity); and (4) stakeholder value associated with perceived opportunity costs (environmental value). The introduction of multiple value dimensions allows for the possibility of overlapping and mutually reinforcing stakeholder values, which fosters stewardship. It is in particular up to the board to articulate, explore and exploit these possibilities of overlap, as these strengthen the commitment and engagement of stakeholders to and with each other and tie the corporate purpose to the realisation of individual purpose. Moreover, while tangible resources and benefits can be finite, possible value overlap is limited to a much smaller extent and can even be mutually reinforcing. Contrary to resource-driven governance configurations, i.e. shareholder and stakeholder governance, in purpose governance, organisations are governed to create congruence (e.g. through business for purpose) among stakeholder values. Consequently, stakeholders depend on the firm and other stakeholders to realise their embedded values. In purpose governance, the board of directors seeks to act as an impartial mediator between the corporate stakeholders to mobilise mutual commitment and engagement and to leverage the potential of embedded stakeholder values (for team production, see also, e.g., Huse and Gabrielsson, 2012). Thus by enacting purpose, corporations are developing 'public good provision' characteristics to the extent that the joint value creation represents (value) attributes that are non-excludable and non-rival. This all is as a consequence of the inclusiveness of the corporation in embracing a larger diversity of private interests across the globe, their contribution to addressing social needs and their direct contribution to the provision of public goods and services in different segments of the world.

This reconfiguration on value attributes instead of free-rider problems makes team production theory a highly relevant perspective for boards of corporations where stakeholders contribute to the firm's corporate purpose and mutually reinforce and co-create stakeholder values and capabilities. The connecting role of the board is vital for the corporation. Boards may emphasise the benefits of inclusion and development of collaborative norms and claim priority for the governance of interaction processes to foster the effective deliberative exchange of information and the finding of joint direction and purpose among stakeholders. Parallel to that is the crucial perspective that human behaviour cannot be purely driven by self-interest. Fostering inclusion implies stepping away from control. Thus, alternative micro-foundations of purpose-driven stakeholder engagement in organisations will build on alternative mixtures of self-realisation and pro-social stakeholder dispositions (see also Bridoux and Stoelhorst, 2014). In line with Bridoux and Stoelhorst (2014), it can be argued that such alternative configurations of governance may trigger stakeholder dispositions through different effects. The first is a sorting effect, as alternative stakeholder dispositions are drawn towards matching governance modes. Attracting stakeholders requires creating accountability and legitimacy. The second is the effect on the intrinsic stakeholder motivation to contribute to the corporate purpose and joint value creation. This requires creating inclusion and deliberation. The combination of sorting and motivational effects will, along the aforementioned lines, foster co-creation of value and purpose within the organisation.

To conclude, the primary role of the board is to guide and guard purpose-driven operations, through the process of creating accountability to and engagement of stakeholders and legitimacy of activities within wider society. Board guidance is provided to stakeholders by engaging them in processes of inclusive deliberation to address and monitor the just balance between the realisation of corporate purpose and the development of individual stakeholder capabilities. To guard requires the board to create accountability and legitimacy of corporate activities related to the corporate purpose towards wider society.

Next to the fundamental ambiguity and equivocality, the complexity and uncertainty of the environment manifests itself in the multiple interdependent relationships and possibly conflicting interests of larger varieties of stakeholders. This multiple-stakeholder perspective addresses secondary uncertainty (such as opportunism) and emphasises the board's role in defining purpose and objectives as influenced by power plays and politics in and between coalitions of relevant stakeholders, including society at large. Purpose governance emphasises the benefits of investing in ongoing high-quality relationships and connections over traditional distant goal alignment. The embeddedness view claims priority for the governance of interaction processes to foster stewardship and the effective exchange and use of information and finding joint direction and purpose among stakeholders.

4.4.2 Purpose-Led Strategy and the Role of the Board

As elaborated in Section 3, the introduction of purpose has important implications for the formation and implementation of strategy. As the purpose of the firm is derived from a broader societal challenge to which the firm contributes in close interaction with others, the strategy of a single firm is embedded in explicit or implicit strategy making by other contributors at the level of networks. Hence, purpose-led strategy is essentially collaborative and not primarily competitive. A solid financial performance by the corporation only serves to realise the set purpose in society. In order to enact purpose, a firm may erase its boundaries and open up to show the resources and competences it has to offer. Given that future unpredictability asks for a transformative approach to strategy making, this is a continuous and ongoing process. Put in the terms of Appleyard and Chesbrough (2017), in this case cooperative value creation never replaces value capture by a single firm. Firms choose and define their corporate purpose to contribute to resolving societal challenges in a meaningful and profitable way. Open, collective, purpose-led strategy making asks for a new repertoire of strategy practices for strategists and boards. Taking the enactment of purpose as leading in corporate strategy implies a perspective on value creation within a value network, building on shared purpose and values, rather than a linear conception of the value chain, with a distinct beginning and end. Purposeful creation of value takes place within an interdependent value network of human intentions and moral agency. Consequently, how to engage stakeholders as partners in enacting purpose becomes the core of strategy. A purpose-driven strategy takes stakeholders, such as customers and suppliers, as partners in value creation, rather than as threats and opportunities (Freeman, Phillips and Sosodia, 2020), and partnering requires reciprocity as much from the focal firm as from the participating stakeholders (Bridoux and Stoelhorst, 2016), implying that perceptions of fairness and equity among stakeholders will impact the efficiency and effectiveness of the interactions in competitive and cooperative contexts.

Our discussion of board roles in Section 4.3 revealed that the involvement of the board in strategy is generally limited to monitoring performance, risk and internal culture and behaviour. This corresponds to most boards taking strategic decisions in situations of risk. As we also mentioned, occasionally boards may be more actively involved in strategy making by offering advice and bringing in relevant connections from their network. Active involvement of boards also pays off with positive effects on strategic change, distinctive choices, firm performance and contribution to social objectives. These board roles have largely been shaped in the context of shareholder governance and are currently subject to change under the influence of the growing number of stakeholders, which is shaping stakeholder governance. However, purpose governance is fundamentally different to the extent that the corporate purpose is only indirectly and limitedly related to the specific interests of shareholders and other stakeholders. Thus, the key question in this section is how the role of boards in strategy is shaped in purpose governance.

Given the complementary and non-exclusive nature of the three strategy roles that McNulty and Pettigrew (1999) distinguish, the board naturally fulfils all three roles – taking strategic decisions, shaping strategic decisions and shaping the content, context and conduct of strategic decisions – in the context of purpose governance. If, for example, the firm's strategy and investments proposed by its management are fully in line with the corporate purpose the firm contributes to, boards can limit their role to taking decisions and only exert their influence at the end of the process. When environmental circumstances are more stable and predictable and allow for strategic planning and positioning (see Wiltbank et al, 2006), active involvement of the board in strategy making can be periodic. Board members will then mainly shape content, context and conduct of strategy making during the stage of strategy formulation. Once the purpose of the firm and its strategies are established, they can take on a more passive role and monitor whether subsequent strategic proposals contribute to the societal purpose pursued by the firm. Incidentally, when new or challenging topics enter the strategic agenda of the firm or rapid adaptation to changing external circumstances is essential, boards may become more active by initiating strategic explorations, driving strategic conversations and activating their network connections to accelerate strategic change. A more active board is also appropriate to support and, when required, challenge visionary leadership. The board may actively intervene when management, contrary to what it assumes, cannot control and shape the context the firm is part of and, as a result, risks overshooting its ambitions.

In general, and more than in shareholder and stakeholder governance, purpose governance requires boards to take on more engaged roles and become actively involved in strategy making. The main reason for this is that in purpose governance, the objectives of the firm broaden from only creating value for shareholders and stakeholders towards contributing to the transformation into sustainable societies, economies and ecologies. As a result, boards are held more responsible towards larger and more diverse groups of stakeholders that are directly and indirectly related to the firm (cf. McNulty, Zattoni and Douglas, 2013; Pugliese, Minichilli and Zattoni, 2014). At the same time, as the boundaries of the firm are fading when business activities become more intricately connected in integrated systems, joint value creation and close collaboration and coordination in strategy making with actors outside of the firm becomes essential (see Bridoux and Stoelhorst, 2014).

The importance of boards in purpose governance being continuously actively involved in strategy making grows further when environmental circumstances are complex and highly unpredictable, yet can be shaped by cooperating closely with actors and institutions that together contribute to the same purpose. It requires joint transformative and open strategy making with all actors and institutions involved. In order to assure cooperation and access to resources, boards have to act as impartial mediators between actors and institutions that are, directly or indirectly, related to the firm (cf. Huse and Gabrielsson, 2012). Building high-quality and ongoing relationships is essential in order to exchange relevant information and find joint direction and purpose among a variety – and, over time, changing constellations – of stakeholders and interest groups. As a result, the main focus of strategy making in purpose governance shifts from a focus on the firm towards its contribution to societal purpose-driven transformation.

In addition, more active involvement of boards in strategy making is also required when the acting management undervalues or underperforms the firm's possible contribution to societal purpose and transformation. Management may still focus too much on firm performance and exploiting existing activities instead of exploring new pathways that contribute to broader, societal purpose in the short or longer term. In order to do so, the firm may need to develop network connections and invest in building innovative ecosystems of which board members are already part and to which they contribute. Boards represent the firm as active members of the purpose-oriented discourse in the broader network and society, being part of realising sustainable transformations and, in doing so, building trust and relationships. Even when management catches up and balances exploitative and explorative contributions to the purpose the firm pursues, the board maintains an active role in strategy making as change, and shaping sustainable transformation is ongoing. Boards are, therefore, leading in transformative strategy making in purpose governance.

Table 7 summarises differences in strategy roles performed by the board in alternative modes of governance. In shareholder governance, the board focuses primarily on ensuring that the company's strategy maximises shareholder return in the short and long term. The more uncertain environmental conditions demand transformational strategy making, the more active the role of the board will be. When required, boards will not hesitate to appoint new management to either increase operational efficiency or explore new strategic routes. In stakeholder governance, as the board extends its focus from shareholder to stakeholder returns, its role changes accordingly. In addition to protecting the

Table 7 Board strategy roles in alternative corporate governance configurations

		Governance configuration		
		Shareholder governance	Stakeholder governance	Purposegovernance
Board strategy role	Taking decisions	Ratification of capital investment proposals in relation to shareholder returns	Monitor alignment of investment proposals with stakeholder interests	Monitor alignment of strategy and transformation with defined corporate purpose
	Shaping decisions	Direct and contribute to the creation and selection of strategic options	Steer strategy making to align with and contribute to stakeholder interests	Bring in new options and competences to co-create and align the purpose and strategy of the firm
	Shaping content, context and conduct of strategy	Lead strategy development and shape the conditions to maximise shareholder returns in the short and longer term.	Lead to create conditions so that stakeholders benefits are continuously part of strategy making	Lead to define purpose as strategy and engage willing stakeholders as partners in building supportive networks to realise transformation

financial interests of shareholders, they passively and actively incorporate stakeholders and their interests in the process of strategy making. The role of the board in strategy making changes more fundamentally under a regime of purpose governance. Given purpose as strategy, the board's focus shifts from the performance of the firm to the purpose to which the firm aims to contribute. Moreover, as purpose implies continuous transformation, the role of the board is both more active and extensive in line with transformative strategy making. Whereas in shareholder and stakeholder governance, the main role of the board is in taking and shaping strategic decisions, in purpose governance, the board continuously plays a leading role in shaping the content, context and conduct of strategy making. Most importantly, the board defines and, when required, redefines the purpose of the firm, concretises it in strategic choices and communicates it to engage willing collaborators inside and outside the firm to realise transformation.

Table 7 does not make a distinction according to the degree of uncertainty of environmental circumstances. As we elaborated on in Section 3.2 following the taxonomy of Wiltbank et al. (2006), effective strategy making varies under different regimes of uncertainty and control. Planning, adaptive, visionary and transformative approaches to strategy making make different assumptions about the predictability and uncertainty of external conditions and the ability to actively influence these. Whereas planning and visionary approaches assume that environmental conditions are rather predictable, adaptive and transformative approaches see it as highly unpredictable and surrounded by major uncertainties and complex dynamics. In addition to the dimension of external predictability, visionary and transformative approaches also assume that firms can actively influence and shape the circumstances they are inherently part of. As environmental conditions may vary, the four approaches to strategy making are complementary, depending on those conditions. They are also all relevant in all modes of governance, depending on the roles boards play, the objectives of the firm and the support and challenging needed by top management.

Table 8 gives an overview of the strategy roles boards play for each approach to strategy making and hence for different degrees of environmental uncertainty and control. The role of the board in purpose governance most closely resembles that in other types of governance when circumstances allow the board to limit their role to taking strategic decisions. As indicated in Section 4.4.2, this is the case when environmental conditions are relatively stable and predictable, and top management is fully aligned and engaged in realising the well-defined purpose of the firm. The main task of the board then is to check and monitor if this is indeed the case and validate the alignment of submitted proposals with

Table 8 Board roles in purpose governance under alternative regimes of uncertainty

		Board strategy role		
		Taking strategic decisions	**Shaping strategic decisions**	**Shaping content, context and conduct of strategic decisions**
Strategy-making approaches in regimes of uncertainty and control	Planning & positioning	Monitor alignment and realisation of strategy with the well-defined corporate purpose	Lead to contribute to defining and realising the purpose and strategy of the firm by exploring new environment options and potential partners	Lead to (re)define purpose and explore new environments, partners and capabilities to find a matching strategy with alternative contexts and engage (new) top executives to implement strategy
	Visioning & creating	Monitor and challenge alignment of vision with the defined purpose of the firm	Lead to introduce new partners and perspectives to challenge, co-create and align purpose, vision and strategy	Lead to define and align purpose and vision of the firm and engage willing collaborators inside and outside the firm
	Adapting & learning	Monitor agility and adaptation of strategy to changing conditions given a set purpose	Lead to reinforce and challenge strategy making to adapt to changing circumstances to realise corporate purpose	Lead to define purpose as strategy to adapt to rapidly changing circumstances
	Transforming & probing	Monitor alignment of strategy and transformation within a defined corporate purpose	Lead to bring in new options, partners and competences to co-create the alignment of purpose and strategy of the firm and support transformation under uncertainty	Lead to define purpose as strategy and engage willing stakeholders as partners to build supportive networks to realise the transformation

the corporate purpose. Incidentally, they may challenge top executives who, in vigorous pursuit of an ambitious vision, risk the continuity of the firm. When environmental uncertainty increases, the board has to make sure that the firm is agile enough and adapts to changing circumstances to realise the corporate purpose. Under transformative strategy making, the board in addition keeps a close eye on top management's efforts and capabilities to actively influence and shape environmental conditions to optimise purpose realisation.

Because pursuing a corporate purpose implies change and transformation, the role of the board in purpose governance is more active and extensive over long periods of time. The active involvement may be by proposing new strategic options and potential partners that contribute to optimising the firm's efforts to realise the purpose. In planning approaches, this includes analysing current and future strategy positions; in visionary approaches, it translates into co-creating the firm's vision. In adaptive planning, the board's efforts focus on learning to adapt to rapidly changing circumstances, while in transformative approaches, it is aimed at shaping the transformation of a firm's strategy and organisation. Whereas, in planning approaches, the board's involvement in strategy making is periodic, in adaptive and transformative approaches, their contribution can be continuous, given uncertain and constantly changing conditions.

When the purpose of the firm needs (re)consideration, the board takes the lead in shaping the content, context and conduct of strategic decisions. The way in which they fulfil this role in the context of purpose governance may vary with the degree of environmental uncertainty. The greater the uncertainty, the more intensive and lasting their involvement is. It is clearly the most extensive in transformative strategy making, when the firm enacts its corporate purpose while manoeuvring in constantly changing circumstances and shaping the future context at the same time. Engaging willing collaborators and appointing committed top executives are an indispensable part of the board's role. Note that the collaborative nature of purpose governance and the active role of boards in this reduces secondary and behavioural uncertainty that under other governance regimes results from opportunistic interactions between competing actors in the value chain to realise the objectives of their shareholders and stakeholders.

4.5 Board Practice and the Governance of Corporate Purpose and Strategy

In purpose-led strategy, the objectives of the firm shift from creating value for shareholders and/or stakeholders towards contributing to societal challenges. This transformation towards sustainable societies, economies and ecologies is continuous and involves collaboration with a broad range of partners across firm boundaries. With purpose becoming strategy, the involvement of the board in strategy increases and moves from taking and shaping strategic decisions towards leading by shaping content, context and conduct of strategic decisions. In a regime of purpose governance, the board can be primarily held accountable for the enactment of the purpose of the firm, next to safeguarding the continuity of the corporation while matching the dispositions of shareholders and other stakeholders. This extended accountability calls for the development of additional practices to be performed by the board.

In this respect, for instance, Younger, Mayer and Eccles (2020) and Huber et al. (2020) describe sets of practices for boards to lead and govern the enactment of the purpose of the firm. Through a much more intense interaction with the relevant environment through search and analysis and scanning for engaged stakeholders, more internally oriented board practices include validating that purpose actually drives strategy and capital-allocation decisions, developing and implementing performance metrics and measures to assess and monitor purpose-driven culture, clearly communicating the purpose of the firm and creating ownership of and engagement with purpose among all stakeholders. In this section, we make a first attempt to integrate and interpret such board practices in purpose governance in the context of the three strategy roles distinguished by McNulty and Pettigrew (1999). In doing so, we differentiate between regimes of risk and uncertainty. To illustrate this exploration, Table 9 gives an overview of board practices in purpose governance under both regimes. Note that board practices in situations of risk and uncertainty are not mutually exclusive with environmental uncertainty creating additional complexity that requires complementary practices from the board to deal with it effectively.

The role of the board in purpose governance can be more at arm's length if the purpose of the firm is well defined and strategic circumstances and outcomes of known alternatives are more predictable, i.e. in situations of risk. To enhance accountability and legitimacy, the board will focus on validating and monitoring the contribution of strategic proposals to realising the purpose of the firm, drawing up consistent performance requirements and remuneration policies for top executives and monitoring a purpose-oriented culture of stakeholders and the possible risks that are involved. Consider, for example, an energy company, whose purpose is to create a more sustainable energy environment for future generations, which has chosen a transition strategy to focus on the production of sustainable energy and has accommodated its long-term investments in line with its strategy and purpose. Relevant board practices include the analysis of societal challenges towards circularity, ensuring the pace of the

Table 9 Board practices in purpose governance

		Board strategy role	
	Taking strategic decisions	**Shaping strategic decisions**	**Shaping content, context and conduct of strategic decisions**
Strategy-making approaches in regimes of uncertainty and control			
Risk	Validate that purpose drives strategy and investment decisions; monitor purpose-driven culture; assess risks involved; validate that performance metrics and compensation agreements are aligned and purpose-driven	Bring in additional expertise to identify and create alternative strategic options and scenarios to enact purpose; develop metrics to assess and track purpose performance and (re) design and develop alternative reward systems	Initiate and facilitate (re)defining the corporate purpose; engage existing stakeholders in deliberative decision-making regarding purpose, strategy and leadership; change membership and partner relationships; consider adjustment of Top Management Team and Board of Directors composition in view of (re)defining purpose
Uncertainty	Validate that foresight and scenario analysis is used to assess the impact on purpose of possible change and	Identify and co-create purpose-driven narratives and experiments; create internal and external legitimacy for	Actively engage new and old stakeholders to reduce uncertainty; absorb environmental uncertainty in

Table 9 (cont.)

	Board strategy role	
Taking strategic decisions	**Shaping strategic decisions**	**Shaping content, context and conduct of strategic decisions**
disruption to challenge top management practices; monitor resilience capacity to safeguard continuity	experiments of stakeholders groups to explore and manage options to foster purpose by absorbing and benefitting from uncertainty	deliberative decision-making on purpose, strategy and leadership; transform the organisation, including TMT and BOD make-up to accommodate new realities; create internal and external accountability and legitimacy for alternative purpose-led pathways

transformation is in line with a well-specified timeline defined by the corporate purpose, the assessment of strategic milestones, the transparent communication of steps to enact purpose to internal and external stakeholders, the validation and effectuation of the associated reward structure and the monitoring and evaluation of possible risks that are involved. Generally, the board aims to hold top management accountable for the realisation of the corporate purpose and the related strategy and to create transparency and legitimacy for engaged internal and external stakeholders.

When the purpose of the firm is clearly defined but the future context is surrounded by major strategic uncertainties and hence, to a greater or lesser extent, unpredictable, evaluation of strategic decisions and creating accountability and legitimacy for corporate activities become more challenging. Board practices may then include the evaluation and validation of strategy and investment proposals against the background of the alternative pathways and scenarios that ecosystems may take and the different speeds at which these may develop. Creating awareness of and monitoring and interpreting early signs of transformation, applying scenario analysis and employing foresight methods to evaluate the impact of possible change and disruption on the enactment of the corporate purpose are essential practices in such situations. To challenge executives in that direction, creating an ongoing dialogue with top management, monitoring the collection of information in a wide network and engaging key stakeholders ensures that executives remain alert to emerging and unexpected developments that might harm the enactment of the corporate purpose. Under uncertainty, such practices enable board effectiveness in providing accountability and legitimacy of the chosen pathways so as to mitigate ambiguity and to maintain transparency towards internal and external stakeholders.

When strategic options to enact the purpose of the firm are still under development or the contribution of options to the stated purpose is not yet fully clear, boards take a more proactive role in shaping strategic direction from the outset. Board members participate in identifying, exploring and developing relevant options and act as a linking pin between the firm and the network it is or needs to be part of. Both specialised expertise and broader network experience can be brought in to fulfil this role. Board members may seek to apply relevant expertise to design the appropriate metrics to measure and monitor sustainable purpose-driven performance, evaluate risk and affordable loss scenarios and validate the design of appropriate incentive systems to ensure and track purposeful accountability by top management (cf. Huber et al., 2020; Younger, Mayer and Eccles 2020). Moreover, as the strategy of the firm in purpose governance is openly co-created and realised, stewardship of stakeholders becomes indispensable. Effective boards know how to connect and involve stakeholders so as to build strong partnerships in a way that the corporate purpose benefits from stakeholder engagement, competences and dispositions. The more uncertain future circumstances and transformations are, the more active and continuous the contribution of the board to strategy becomes. In addition to the aforementioned practices they perform when shaping strategic decisions, identifying and developing options to manage, absorb or benefit from uncertainty and connecting new coalitions of co-creating stakeholders emerge as core board practices. Rather than designing concrete activities, the emphasis will be on the development of the narrative that engages stakeholders and integrates a rich diversity of perspectives that can be transformed into an explorative set of initiatives. Thus, the internal and external pressures on corporations to actively contribute to broader social goals as exemplified in the corporate purpose shapes corporations as 'polities' consisting of multiple interest groups, distributions of stakeholder rights and duties and governance systems that need to be proactively directed by the board, in particular in situations of fundamental uncertainty (Aguilera et al., 2007).

By expanding their role from taking to shaping strategic decisions, boards become more actively and continuously involved in purpose-led strategy making. In particular, it requires board members to bring in capabilities in connecting engaged stakeholders to actively advance the purpose of the firm. In a regime of uncertainty, this involvement becomes even more intense. However, when shaping the content, context and conduct of strategy, boards take a leading role in strategy and purpose. Compared to shareholder and stakeholder governance, in purpose governance, the efforts of the board radically shift from a focus on the firm itself towards the societal context and the purposeful contribution to society the firm endeavours to make. Note that this stretches the concept of open strategy as introduced by Chesbrough and Appleyard (2006) from a thoughtful, possibly temporary, choice by a stand-alone firm to an ongoing, collaborative purpose and strategy-making endeavour with internal and external stakeholders as partners. This, in particular, is the context where deliberative decision-making comes to the fore, to the extent that the board will lead or direct the process of the joint establishment of purpose and strategy and the resulting allocation of decision rights in terms of governance. This regime introduces the corporation as a political actor in wider society, connecting engaged stakeholders to enacting a jointly shaped or reshaped purpose. By collaborating on societal challenges, in the regime of purpose governance, firms emerge as active social players and corporate citizens (Matten and Crane, 2005). Palazzo and Scherer (2008) argue for labelling corporations as political actors to emphasise that both public and private actors are involved in multilevel governance networks. Scherer, Baumann-Pauly and Schneider (2012) point to the democratic deficit that emerges when hierarchically governed corporations engage in public policymaking, either by claiming citizenship rights and providing public goods (i.e. corporate citizenship) or by influencing the political system and lobbying for their economic interests (i.e. strategic corporate political activities). Addressing the deficit asks for a broader political perspective on the corporate governance of the corporation. To create and realise the corporate purpose, the board's role is to internalise democratic decision-making and engage committed stakeholders in the actual governance of the corporation. The board may facilitate (formally or informally) the development of an issue arena that functions as the focal place where stakeholders coordinate collective actions, reinforce shared interests and facilitate 'stake exchange' (see Luoma-Aho and Vos, 2010). To create accountability and engagement, identifying and engaging willing and supportive stakeholders as collaborative partners in deciding on the purpose and strategy of the firm develops as the core activity of the board. Connecting and committing willing stakeholders around a shared purpose facilitates alignment and coordination of collective actions, reduces behavioural uncertainty and absorbs environmental uncertainty through collaboration in actively shaping the environment. If the joint process of creating and articulating shared purpose does not resolve conflicts between stakeholders, boards mediate between stakeholders whose interests and objectives conflict to reduce behavioural uncertainty from opportunistic interactions. When stakeholders partner in such purpose-driven value networks, stakeholder relationships will be reciprocal (cf. Freeman et al., 2020). The board of the focal firm safeguards the joint interest, i.e. corporate purpose, of all stakeholders and is accountable as such. This board can be structured as fiduciary decision-making or embedded in shared decision-making (Zeitoun, Osterloh and Frey, 2014). By fiduciary decision-making, the board of directors has the fiduciary duty to act in the best interest of the corporate purpose. In order to do so, potential competing claims from stakeholders are addressed and resolved by benchmarking against the corporate purpose (see Section 3). Alternatively, interdependencies can be created among stakeholders through boundary spanning by co-opting stakeholders in processes of deliberative decision-making as mediated by the board (see Harrison and St John, 1996: 48–52). Co-opting stakeholders in these deliberations opens possibilities for shared decision-making about purpose and purpose-led strategy. The board may develop into several compound boards to accommodate the input and participation of stakeholders into actual deliberation and decision-making. In particular, in situations where complexity and uncertainty is prevalent, granting decision rights to multiple stakeholders, for example through creating compound boards, opens the possibility of embracing or adapting to fundamental uncertainty (see Turnbull, 2012).

5 Discussion, Reflection and Research Agenda

This Element has analysed the implications for strategy and corporate governance of the shift towards purpose-driven business activities. Defining corporate purpose as the fundamental and unique contribution of the corporation to the world at large, purpose implies first and foremost exploring the outside world in many aspects so as to define as precisely as possible which contribution the corporation is committed to make. Subsequently, this contribution needs to be reflected in its for-profit business activities before it can be credibly communicated to the outside world. Developing purpose thus implies adjustment of portfolio and strategy, redefining culture and relationships, adapting process and systems and introducing new performance and activity metrics. Furthermore, for corporate governance, the introduction of corporate purpose has fundamental implications. Corporate purpose elevates the reason for the existence of the corporation beyond the objectives of stakeholders. Indeed, where corporate governance is traditionally concerned with stakeholders' interest and the allocation of corporate returns to stakeholders, in purpose governance, the role of corporate governance is directed towards the enactment of corporate purpose. Thus, in this configuration, board members first and foremost direct their attention towards the firm and its purpose itself and secondarily towards the implications for alternative stakeholder interests. This direction reestablishes the relevance of external engagement, revision of external positions and affiliation with stakeholders as important elements of corporate governance, next to aligning purpose with governance decisions related to compensation, shareholder reward, customer expectations and employee job security. It is our contention that research into the nature of corporate governance in view of the introduction of corporate purpose as the reason for the existence of the firm has only just started.

Next to purpose, the Element has emphasised the importance of incorporating the complexity and fundamental uncertainty of the current (business) environment. The recognition of our fundamental lack of knowledge and understanding of the world also has important implications for our thinking about the governance of corporations. According to the currently dominant paradigm, a well-functioning corporate governance regime has a positive impact on the corporation's results in two ways – it lowers both the contract and the agency costs, which implies that firm-specific investments can be better utilised. In this Element, it is argued that this paradigm fits within a limited, linear perspective on a complex and uncertain world. The illusion of 'in control' is limited to the boundaries of the control framework (governance bundle) that is created. Often, this illusion is supported by self-reinforcing dynamics (habits of control), wherein considerations regarding the efficiency of the current system are overemphasised at the neglect of considerations regarding the increased fragility of the system itself. Emergent patterns can suddenly change the regime characteristics and permanently disrupt the apparent robustness or fitness of the system. Resilient corporations are alert to such changes and can adapt, precisely because of the resilience and creativity of the organisation and its governance structure. By doing so, the continuity and fitness of the corporations can be assured. Rather than emphasising control, the robustness of long-term resilience of corporations is safeguarded through learning capabilities, adaptability and reaching out to the wider (business) environment through sharing ideas, co-creation of experiments and building shared narratives. It is the role of the board to develop the conditions for such sustainable processes of value creation and purpose enactment. More specifically, the role of the board is to actively work on safeguarding ambidexterity and nourishing network connections with multiple stakeholders, facilitating information collection and alertness to weak signals, stimulating experimentation and shaping the purpose and agenda for the future long-term sustainability of the corporation. To advance understanding, more detailed case-based research in particular into the roles the board has in building resilience and agility is required.

The contribution of the Element to the extant literature of board and corporate governance is to revisit in more detail the active involvement of the board in purpose and strategy to cope with the complex and uncertain environment. By explicitly acknowledging the distinction between risk and uncertainty in a complex business environment, the Element makes an attempt to develop a conceptual framework for the strategy role of the board in social systems characterised by complexity and uncertainty, by combining these dimensions with McNulty and Pettigrew's typology of the strategic role of the board. Effective boards safeguard the challenging (dynamic) balance between exploitation and exploration in strategic decision-making. In exploitation, the board creates accountability through complexity reduction by emphasising control and incremental decision-making, to create transparency of decision-making and involve stakeholders. Exploration is aimed at absorption of the complexity of the environment through sharing decision-making authority in deliberative processes, stimulating search and alertness, experimenting and shared learning, facilitating risk taking, developing resilience and increasing adaptability. In this respect, the relevance of a larger multiplicity of stakeholders, possibly characterised by diverse and perhaps conflicting sets of demands on the corporation, needs recognition. It requires from the board more intense network activities and the organisation of participatory decision-making systems.

Embracing purpose implies that the question of corporate governance changes from 'for whom the corporation created value' to 'for what (purpose) the corporation produces value' (Levillain and Segrestin, 2019: 641). In line with this, the focus of attention not only includes the contribution of the firm to stakeholders but also stakeholders' contribution to the firm and its purpose (see also Bacq and Aguilera, 2021). Thus, the governance problem is no longer only one in which stakeholder interests provide 'primacy' and ultimate decision rights. Instead, the governance challenge is also to create purpose commitment among all stakeholders. In this respect, purpose becomes both an attractor and a self-selection mechanism for corporate stakeholders. Honouring the commitment to purpose does require attention to stakeholder interest and opportunities but always in the context of purpose enactment. Additional conceptual and theory-informed research may help to understand the fundamental problems of purpose governance and purpose commitment of relevant stakeholders in relation to interest alignment and a fair distribution of benefits and opportunities.

The introduction of shared and purpose-led strategic decision-making within the board may not be possible without reconsidering the make-up of the board. Indeed, it can be concluded that, with the role of the board in strategy changing from a passive observer at a distance to an involved key player in shaping the content, context and conduct of strategy, thoughts on the make-up of the board need attention. The institutional reality is still that boards across the globe are fairly uniform and characterised by low diversity. A question that arises is whether the current archetypical make-up and role of the board matches the complexity and challenges of the twenty-first century and the purpose-oriented reconfiguration of the corporation and its governance. It is intriguing to explore how the challenges and increased complexity of board roles may have implications for the make-up of boards. For instance, it can be speculated as to whether the emphasis on dynamic capabilities (Teece, 2007), strategic engagement and enactment of purpose imply a more ongoing reconfiguration of the board itself as 'the apex of the organisation'. First of all, a larger diversity of board members is helpful in exploring, understanding and anticipating the complex reality (see Hoppmann, Naegele and Girod, 2019). Second, it may be proposed that, from the point of view of the legitimation of strategic activities, a more active involvement of external stakeholders in decision-making and action is important and may help in responding to the complex social demands on the corporation. Both developments include an active dialogue and the organisation of deliberative decision-making and shaping together with stakeholders. Boards may proactively access the networks of stakeholders and inquire about important dilemmas and actions expected from the corporation. The need for such decentralised forms of consultation makes the role of the board in shaping context, content and conduct more relevant for exploring the future of the corporation. It requires interaction with the wider network and engagement with demands from external stakeholders in the boardroom to create accountability and legitimacy. It may suggest a more political perspective on board dynamics (Ravasi and Zattoni, 2006). Involving stakeholders in the firm's governance is also underlined by Schrage et al. (2021), who in developing the concept of a purpose gap underscore the relevance of aligning purpose, strategy and values among leaders and stakeholders. A purpose gap may imply that corporate leadership lacks credibility in aligning their organisations with a shared strategy to realise the purpose. The potential lack of credibility may suggest additional research into board dynamics, in particular the study of interactions between board members and engaged stakeholders.

Turning to the structuring of the board, contrary to the current hierarchical model, an extensive network governance model may be better aligned with the complex pressures and uncertainty of the twenty-first-century business environment. To enable access to and dialogue with stakeholders, the current board structure could be broken down into several core decision-making groups, some groups with a formal fiduciary task and others structuring the network of non-core members within a wider distribution of decision rights, so as to provide more scope for an active exploration of purpose and matching strategic opportunities and challenges. Perhaps such restructuring can be organised through board committees or the establishment of a plurality of parity boards with separated responsibilities and tasks. Also, more radical expansions of distributing decision rights towards a variety of alternative stakeholder councils can be considered. Williamson (1996) already introduced several board configurations to accommodate more extensive stakeholder involvement in order to secure their stake in terms of asset specificity, such as mixed boards with pro rata stakes for stakeholders and specialised boards in which specific stakeholder groups might form the board and others may have an observer status assigned to them to permit their specialised advice or to satisfy their informational needs (Williamson, 1996: 313–14). To illustrate the compound board or network governance, Pirson and Turnbull (2012) point to the participatory governance structure of Mondragon Cooperative Enterprises as a best practice of wider stakeholder involvement. Grandori (2016) argues that, in the context of knowledge intensive work and human capital assets, a more democratic allocation of decision rights allows for governing relationships with associating members of a partnership who invest their capital (human or financial) for generating value in varying formats (direct or indirect, one head, one vote or weighted by investment). Finally, Zeitoun,

Osterloh and Frey (2014) suggest a dual-chamber board to enable the involvement of all stakeholders making non-contractable firm-specific investments. Future empirical research into the efficacy of existing alternative board configurations, also including boards outside the corporate sector, can be recommended to advance understanding of the make-up and role of board configurations in view of the complexity and challenges of the twenty-first century and the purpose-oriented reconfiguration of the corporation and its governance.

Ultimately, corporate governance is concerned with the allocation of decision rights, or as we have defined in Section 1, the creation and allocation of power and influence over decision-making about the control and direction of the corporation (Aguilera and Jackson, 2010). Mainstream shareholder and stakeholder corporate governance has developed this allocation from the concept of residual right of control, i.e. corporate governance is seen as complementing those rights that due to incompleteness could not be formally contracted. As such, shareholder primacy has been motivated by the assessment of non-contractable claims on the value of corporations. And similarly, critiques of shareholder primacy have revolved around the argument that shareholders cannot be regarded as the only residual claimants of the corporation. Thus, the theoretical justification of existing corporate governance is built on the protection of stakeholder rights that cannot be formally contracted. To some extent, the introduction of purpose governance is breaking with this line of argument, since the ultimate focus of corporate governance is not on safeguarding the interests or (residual) claims of participating stakeholders but on the corporation and the enactment of its purpose as such. This corporate purpose cannot be regarded as a residual claim; neither can a joint corporate purpose be directly derived from specific individual-stakeholder interests. For corporate governance in general, this may imply that there is a need for a reformulation of its (theoretical) foundation and legitimate appearance. For board effectiveness, this implies a fundamental reconsideration of the role boards may have in corporate governance. To some extent, the fundamental starting point – that boards act in the interest of the corporation – gains in relevance, since the existence of the corporation can no longer be seen as independent from the societal challenges that motivate its ultimate reason for existence. It provides the board discretion, yet at the same time it is a discretion that requires ongoing interaction and deliberation to create accountability and legitimacy from the outside environment. The role of the board in strategy and purpose is to engage all those affected by the corporate purpose, not only those that hold a stake but all constituencies that have a right in the enactment of the corporate purpose. How to design structures, systems, processes and actions that make boards effective in such roles reflects an important subject for additional research.

References

Ackoff, R. L. (1970). *A Concept of Corporate Planning*, New York: Wiley.

Adner, R. & Kapoor, R. (2010). Value creation in innovation ecosystems: How the structure of technological interdependence affects firm performance in new technology generations. *Strategic Management Journal*, 31(3), 306–33.

Aguilera, R. V. & Jackson, G. (2010). Comparative and international corporate governance. *The Academy of Management Annals*, 4(1), 485–556.

Aguilera, R. V., Rupp, D. E., Williams, C. A. & Ganapathi, J. (2007), Putting the S back in corporate social responsibility: A multi-level theory of social change in organizations. *Academy of Management Review*, 32(3), 836–63.

Aldrich, H. E. & Ruef, M. (2006). *Organizations Evolving*, London: Sage.

Altman, E. J. & Tushman, M. L. (2017). *Platforms, Open/User Innovation, and Ecosystems: A Strategic Leadership Perspective*, Harvard Business School Organizational Behavior Unit, Working Paper No. 17–076.

Andrews, K. R. ([1971] 1980). *The Concept of Corporate Strategy*, Homewood, IL: Irwin.

Ansoff, H. I. (1965). *Corporate Strategy*, New York: McGraw-Hill.

Appleyard, M. M. & Chesbrough, H. W. (2017). The dynamics of open strategy: From adoption to reversion. *Long Range Planning*, 50(3), 310–21.

Argenti, J. (1980). *Practical Corporate Planning*, London: George Allen & Unwin.

Argote, L. & Greve, H. R. (2007). *A Behavioral Theory of the Firm* – 40 years and counting: Introduction and impact. *Organization Science*, 18(3), 337–49.

Arthur, W. B. (1991). *Complexity and the Economy*, Oxford: Oxford University Press.

Arthur, W. B. (1999). Complexity and the economy. *Science*, 284(5411), 107–9.

Arthurs, J. D. & Busenitz, L. W. (2003). The boundaries and limitations of agency theory and stewardship theory in the venture capitalist/entrepreneur relationship. *Entrepreneurship Theory and Practice*, 28(2), 145–62.

Autio, E. & Thomas, L. D. W. (2014). Innovation ecosystems: Implications for innovation management. In M. Dodgson, N. Philips and D. M. Gann, eds., *The Oxford Handbook of Innovation Management*. Oxford: Oxford University Press, 204–28.

Bacq, S. & Aguilera, R. V. (2021). Stakeholder governance for responsible innovation: A theory of value creation, appropriation, and distribution. *Journal of Management Studies*, 59(1), 29–60.

Bailey, B. C. & Peck, S. I. (2013). Boardroom strategic decision-making style: Understanding the antecedents. *Corporate Governance: An International Review*, 21(2), 131–46.

Bartlett, C. A. & Ghoshal, S. (1994). Changing the role of top management: Beyond purpose to strategy. *Harvard Business Review*, 72(6), 79–88.

Becht., M., Bolton, P. & Röell, A. (2002). *Corporate Governance and Control*, National Bureau of Economic Research, Working Paper 9371.

Benkler, Y. & Nissenbaum, H. (2006). Commons-based peer production and virtue. *Journal of Political Philosophy*, 14(4), 394–419.

Birkinshaw, J. (2017). Reflections on open strategy. *Long Range Planning*, 50 (1), 423–6.

Blair, M. M. (2004). Ownership and control: Rethinking corporate governance for the twenty-first century. In T. Clarke, ed., *Theories of Corporate Governance: The Philosophical Foundations of Corporate Governance*. London: Routledge, pp. 174–88.

Blair, M. M. & Stout, L. A. (1999). A team production theory of corporate law. *Virginia Law Review*, 85(2), 247–328.

Boivie, S., Bednar, M. K., Aguilera, R. V. & Andrus, J. L. (2016). Are boards designed to fail? The implausibility of effective board monitoring. *Academy of Management Annals*, 10(1), 319–407.

Bridoux, F. & Stoelhorst, J. W. (2014). Microfoundations for stakeholder theory: Managing stakeholders with heterogeneous motives. *Strategic Management Journal*, 35(1), 107–25.

Bridoux, F. & Stoelhorst, J. W. (2016). Stakeholder relationships and social welfare: A behavioral theory of contributions to joint value creation. *Academy of Management Review*, 41(2), 229–51.

Business Roundtable (2018, 2019). *Statement on the Purpose of the Corporation*. Retrieved from www.businessroundtable.org.

Chaffee, E. E. (1985). Three models of strategy. *The Academy of Management Review*, 10(1), 89–98.

Chandler, A. D. (1962). *Strategy and Structure: Chapters in the History of the Industrial Enterprise*, Cambridge, MA: MIT Press.

Chesbrough, H. W. & Appleyard, M. M. (2006). Open innovation and strategy. *California Management Review*, 50(1), 57–76.

Christensen, C. M. (1997). *The Innovator's Dilemma: When New Technologies Cause Great Firms to Fail*, Boston, MA: Harvard Business School Press.

Collins, J. C. & Porras, J. I. (1994). *Built to Last: Successful Habits of Visionary Companies*, New York: Harper Business.

Cyert, R. M. (1988). *The Economic Theory of Organization and the Firm*, New York: Harvester-Wheatsheaf.

Cyert, R. M. & March, J. G. (1959). Satisfactory profits as a guide to firm behavior. *The Quarterly Journal of Economics*, 73(4), 684–5.

Cyert, R. M. & March, J. G. (1963). *A Behavioral Theory of the Firm*, Englewood Cliffs, NJ: Prentice Hall.

Dahlmann, F. & Brammer, S. (2011). Exploring and explaining patterns of adaptation and selection in corporate environmental strategy in the USA. *Organization Studies*, 32(4), 527–53.

Davis, G. (2016). Can an economy survive without corporations? Technology and robust organizational alternatives. *Academy of Management Perspectives*, 30(2), 129–40.

Davis, J. P., Eisenhardt, K. M. & Bingham, C. B. (2009). Optimal structure, market dynamism, and the strategy of the simple rules. *Administrative Science Quarterly*, 54(3), 413–52.

Davis, J. P., Schoorman, F. D. & Donaldson, L. (1997). Toward a stewardship theory of management. *Academy of Management Review*, 22(1), 20–47.

Dew, N., Read, S., Sarasvathy, S. D. & Wiltbank, R. (2008). Outlines of a behavioral theory of the entrepreneurial firm. *Journal of Economic Behavior and Organization*, 66(1), 37–59.

Donaldson, T. & Davis, J. H. (1991). Stewardship theory or agency theory: CEO governance and shareholder returns. *Australian Journal of Management*, 16 (1), 49–64.

Drucker, P. (1954). *The Practice of Management*, New York: HarperCollins Publishers.

Duncan, R. B. (1972). Characteristics of organizational environments and perceived environmental uncertainty. *Administrative Science Quarterly*, 17 (3), 313–27.

Durand, R., Grant, R. M. & Madsen, T. L. (2017). The expanding domain of strategic management research and the quest for integration. *Strategic Management Journal*, 38(1), 4–16.

Fama, E. F. & Jensen, M. C. (1983). Separation of ownership and control. *The Journal of Law and Economics*, 26(2), 301–25.

Forbes, D. P. & Milliken, F. (1999). Cognition and corporate governance: Understanding boards of directors as strategic decision-making groups. *Academy of Management Review*, 24(2), 489–505.

Foss., N. J. (2001). Bounded rationality in the economics of organization: Present use and (some) future possibilities. *Journal of Management and Governance*, 5(3/4), 401–25.

Freeman, R. E. (1984). *Strategic Management: A Stakeholder Approach*, Boston, MA: Pitman.

Freeman, R. E., Phillips, R. and Sisodia, R. (2020). Tensions in stakeholder theory. *Business and Society*, 59(2), 213–31.

Galbraith, J. R. (1973). *Designing Complex Organizations*, Reading, MA: Addison-Wesley.

Gartenberg, C., Prat, A. & Serfeim, G. (2019). Corporate purpose and financial performance. *Organization Science*, 30(1), 1–18.

Golden, B. R. & Zajac, E. J. (2001). When will boards influence strategic change? Inclination × power = strategic change. *Strategic Management Journal*, 22(12), 1087–111.

Gond, J.-P., O'Sullivan, N., Slager, R., Homanen, M. & Mosony, S. (2018). How ESG engagement creates value for investors and companies. Principles for Responsive Investment, United Nations Global Compact.

Goold, M. & Campbell, A. (1987). *Strategies and Styles: The Role of the Center in Managing Diversified Corporations*, Oxford: Blackwell.

Goold, M., Campbell, A. & Alexander, M. (1994). *Corporate-Level Strategy: Creating Value in the Multi-Business Company*, New York: Wiley.

Gordon, J. R. (1993). *A Diagnostic Approach to Organizational Behavior*, 4th ed., Needham Heights, MA: Allyn and Bacon.

Grandori, A. (2016). Knowledge intensive work and the (re)emergence of democratic governance. *Academy of Management Perspectives*, 30(2), 167–81.

Guillen, M. F. & Ontiveros, E. (2016). *Global Turning Points: Understanding the Challenges for Business in the 21st Century*, Cambridge: Cambridge University Press.

Hambrick, D. C. & Fredrickson, J. W. (2001). Are you sure you have a strategy? *Academy of Management Executive*, 15(4), 48–59.

Hamel, G. & Prahalad, C. K. (1989). Strategic intent. *Harvard Business Review*, 67(3), 63–76.

Harrison, J. S. & St John, C. H. (1996). Managing and partnering with external stakeholders. *Academy of Management Executive*, 10(2), 46–60.

Harrison, J. S. & Wicks, A. C. (2013). Stakeholder theory, value, and firm performance. *Business Ethics Quarterly*, 23(1), 97–124.

Haynes, K. T. & Hillman, A. (2010). The effect of board capital and CEO power on strategic change. *Strategic Management Journal*, 31(11), 1145–63.

Helfat, C. E. & Teece, D. J. (1987). Vertical integration and risk reduction. *Journal of Law and Economics*, 3(1), 47–67.

Henderson, B. D. (1979). *Henderson on Corporate Strategy*, Cambridge, MA: Abt Books.

Hendry, J. (2002). The principals' other problems: Honest incompetence and management contracts. *Academy of Management Review*, 27(1), 98–113.

Hendry, J. (2005). Beyond self-interest: Agency theory and the board in a satisficing world. *British Journal of Management*, 16(1), S55–S63.

Hollensbe, E., Wookey, C., Hickey, L., George, G. & Nichols, C. V. (2014). Organizations with purpose. *Academy of Management Journal*, 57(5), 1227–34.

Hoppman, J., Naegele, F. & Girod, B. (2019). Boards as a source of inertia: Examining the internal challenges and dynamics of boards and directors in times of environmental discontinuities. *Academy of Management Journal*, 62 (2), 437–68.

Huber, C., Leape, S., Mark, L. & Simpson, B. (2020). The board's role in embedding corporate purpose: Five actions directors can take today. Downloaded November 2020 from McKinsey & Company: www.mckinsey.com/business-functions/strategy-and-corporate-finance/our-insights/the-boards-role-in-embedding-corporate-purpose-five-actions-directors-can-take-today.

Huse, M. (2007). *Boards, Governance and Value Creation: The Human Side of Corporate Governance*, Cambridge: Cambridge University Press.

Huse, M. (2009). *The Value Creating Board*, New York: Routledge.

Huse, M. & Gabrielsson, J. (2012). Board leadership and value creation: An extended team production approach. In T. Clarke and D. Branson, eds., T. Clarke and D. Branson, eds.,*Handbook of Corporate Governance*. London & Thousand Oaks, CA:: Sage, pp. 233–52.

Huse, M. & Rindova, V. P. (2001). Stakeholders' expectations of board roles: The case of subsidiary boards. *Journal of Management and Governance*, 5 (2), 153–78.

Ingley, C. B. & Van der Walt, N. T. (2001). The strategic board: The changing role of directors in developing and monitoring corporate capability. *Corporate Governance*, 9(3), 174–85.

Jarzabkowski, P. (2007). An activity-theory approach to strategy as practice. In D. Golsorkhi, L. Rouleau, D. Seidl and E. Vaara, eds., *Cambridge Handbook of Strategy as Practice*. Cambridge: Cambridge University Press, pp. 127–40.

Jarzabkowski, P., Balogun, J. & Seidl, B. (2007). Strategizing: The challenges of a practice perspective. *Human Relations*, 60(1), 5–27.

Jarzabkowski, P. & Spee, A. P. (2009). Strategy-as-practice: A review and future directions for the field. *International Journal of Management Reviews*, 11(1), 69–95.

Jarzabowski, P. & Whittington, R. (2008). Hard to disagree, mostly. *Strategic Organization*, 6(1), 101–6.

Jensen, M. C. & Meckling, W. H. (1976). Theory of the firm: Managerial behavior, agency cost and ownership structure. *Journal of Financial Economics*, 3(4), 305–60.

Jensen, M. C. & Zajac, E. J. (2004). Corporate elites and corporate strategy: how demographic preferences and structural position shape the scope of the firm. *Strategic Management Journal*, 25(6), 507–24.

Johnson, G. (1987). *Strategic Change and the Management Process*, Oxford: Blackwell.

Johnson, G., Melin, L. & Whittington, R. (2003). Micro strategy and strategizing: Towards an activity-based view. *Journal of Management Studies*, 40(1), 3–22.

Johnson, J. L., Daily, C. M. & Ellstrand, A. E. (1996). Boards of directors: A review and research agenda. *Journal of Management*, 22(3), 409–38.

Kaplan, R. S. & Norton, D. P. (2004). *Strategy Maps: Converting Intangible Assets into Tangible Outcomes*, Boston, MA: Harvard Business School Press.

Kaufman, A. & Englander, E. (2011). Behavioral economics, federalism, and the triumph of stakeholder theory, *Journal of Business Ethics*, 102(3), 421–38.

Kendry, K. & Kiel, G. C. (2004). The role of the board in firm strategy: Integrating agency and organizational control perspectives. *Corporate Governance*, 12(4), 500–20.

Klein, P. G., Mahoney, J. T., McGahan, A. M. & Pitelis, C. N. (2012). Who is in charge? A property rights perspective on stakeholder governance. *Strategic Organization*, 10(3), 304–15.

Klein, P. G., Mahoney, J. T., McGahan, A. M. & Pitelis, C. N. (2019). Organizational governance adaptation: Who is in, who is out, and who gets what. *Academy of Management Review*, 44(1), 6–27.

Knight, F. H. (1921). *Risk, Uncertainty and Profit*, Boston, MA: Houghton Mifflin.

Koontz, H. & O'Donnell, C. (1959). *Principles of Management: An Analysis of Managerial Functions*, 2nd ed., New York: McGraw Hill.

Koopmans, T. C. (1957). *Three Essays on the State of Economic Science*, New York: McGraw Hill.

Levillain, K. & Segrestin, B. (2019). From primacy to purpose commitment: How emerging profit-with-purpose corporations open new corporate governance avenues. *European Management Journal*, 37(5), 637–47.

Levinthal, D. & March, J. G. (1993). The myopia of learning. *Strategic Management Journal*, 14(2), 95–112.

Lindblom, C. E. (1959). The science of muddling through. *Public Administration Review*, 19(2), 79–88.

Luoma-Aho, V. & Vos, M. (2010). Towards a more dynamic stakeholder model: acknowledging multiple issue arenas. *Corporate Communications: An International Journal*, 15(3), 315–31.

Mace, M. (1971). *Directors: Myth and Reality*, Boston, MA: Harvard Business School Press.

March, J. G. (1962). The business as a political coalition. *Journal of Politics*, 24 (4), 662–78.

March, J. G. (1991). Exploration and exploitation in organizational learning. *Organization Science*, 2(1), 71–87.

March, J. G. (1994). *A Primer on Decision Making: How Decisions Happen*, New York: Free Press.

March, J. G. & Simon, H. A. (1958). *Organizations*, New York: Wiley.

Mason, R. O. & Mitroff, I. (1981). *Challenging Strategic Planning Assumptions*, New York: Wiley.

Matten, D. & Crane, A. (2005). Corporate citizenship: Toward an extended theoretical conceptualization. *Academy of Management Review*, 30(1), 166–79.

Mayer, C. (2016). Reinventing the corporation. *Journal of the British Academy*, 4, 53–72.

Mayer, C., Wright, M. & Phan, P. (2017). Management research and the future of the corporation: A new agenda. *Academy of Management Perspectives*, 31 (3), 179–82.

McGrath, R. G. & Macmillan, I. C. (1995). Discovery driven planning. *Harvard Business Review*, 73(4), 44–54.

McKinsey (2016). Toward a value-creating board. Downloaded January 2021 from McKinsey & Company: www.mckinsey.com/business-functions/strategy-and-corporate-finance/our-insights/toward-a-value-creating-board.

McNulty, T. & Nordberg, D. (2016). Ownership, activism and engagement: Institutional investors as active owners. *Corporate Governance: An international Review*, 24(3), 346–58.

McNulty, T. & Pettigrew, A. (1999). Strategists on the board. *Organization Studies*, 20(1), 47–74.

McNulty, T., Zattoni, A. & Douglas, T. (2013). Developing corporate governance research through qualitative methods: A review of previous studies. *Corporate Governance: An International Review*, 21(2), 183–98.

Miller, D. & Friesen, P. H. (1983). Strategy-making and environment, the third link. *Strategic Management Journal*, 4(3), 221–35.

Milliken, F. J. (1987). Three types of perceived uncertainty about the environment: State, effect, and response uncertainty. *The Academy of Management Review*, 12(1), 133–43.

Mintzberg, H. (1978). Patterns in strategy formation. *Management Science*, 24 (9), 937–48.

Mintzberg H. (1987). Crafting strategy. *Harvard Business Review*, 65(4), 66–75.

Mintzberg, H. (1990). The design school: Reconsidering the basic premises of strategic management. *Strategic Management Journal*, 11(3), 171–95.

Mintzberg, H. (1994). *The Rise and Fall of Strategic Planning*, New York: Free Press.

Mintzberg, H., Ahlstrand, B. W. & Lampel, J. (2009). *Strategy Safari: Your Complete Guide Through the Wilds of Strategic Management*, Harlow: Pearson Education.

Mintzberg, H. & Waters, J. A. (1985). Of strategies, deliberate and emergent. *Strategic Management Journal*, 6(3), 257–72.

Monks, R. A. G. & Minow, N. (2004). *Corporate Governance*, Chichester: Wiley.

Nelson, R. R. & Winter, S. G. (1982). *An Evolutionary Theory of Economic Change*, Boston, MA: Harvard University Press.

Ocasio, W. (1999). Institutionalized action and corporate governance: The reliance on rules of CEO succession. *Administrative Science Quarterly*, 44 (2), 384–416.

Palazzo, G. & Scherer, A. G. (2008). Corporate social responsibility, democracy, and the politicization of the corporation. *Academy of Management Review*, 33(3), 773–5.

Patvardhan, S. & Ramachandran, J. (2020). Shaping the future: Strategy making as an artificial evolution. *Organization Science*, 31(3), 671–97.

Pearce, J. A., II (1995). A structural analysis of dominant coalitions in small banks. *Strategic Management Journal*, 21(6), 1075–95.

Pettigrew, A. M. (1985). *The Awakening Giant*, Oxford: Blackwell.

Pfeffer, J. & Salancik, G. R. (1978). *The External Control of Organizations: A Resource Dependence Perspective*, New York: Harper and Row.

Pirson, M. & Turnbull, S. (2012). Complexity theory, CSR, and corporate governance: The need for alternative governance models, Humanistic Management Research Paper 14/04.

Porter, M. E. (1980). *Competitive Strategies: Techniques for Analyzing Industries and Competitors*, New York: Free Press.

Porter, M. E. (1985). *Competitive Advantage: Creating and Sustaining Superior Performance*, New York: Free Press.

Porter, M. E. (1996). What is strategy? *Harvard Business Review*, 74(6), 61–80.

Postma, T. J. B. M. (1989). 'Strategische Beslissingsprocessen in Ziekenhuizen: Een Casebenadering (Strategic Decision Processes in Hospitals: A Case Approach)', unpublished PhD thesis, University of Groningen.

Postma, T. J. B. M. & Bood, R. P. (2015). Behavioral governance: The role of scenario thinking in dealing with strategic uncertainty. In T. K. Das, ed., *The*

Practice of Behavioral Strategy. Charlotte: Information Age Publishing, pp. 41–75.

Pugliese, A., Bezemer, P., Zattoni, A., Huse, M., Van den Bosch, H. & Volberda, H. W. (2009). Boards of directors' contribution to strategy: A literature review and research agenda. *Corporate Governance, An International Review,* 17(3), 292–306.

Pugliese, A., Minichilli, A. & Zattoni, A. (2014). Integrating agency and resource dependency theory: Firm profitability, industry regulation & board task performance. *Journal of Business Research,* 67(6), 1189–200.

Quinn, J. B. (1980). *Strategies for Change: Logical Incrementalism,* Homewood, IL: Irwin.

Raisch, S. & Tushman, M. L. (2016). Growing new corporate businesses: From initiation to graduation. *Organization Science,* 27(5), 1237–57.

Rajan, R. G. & Zingales, L. (1998). Power in a theory of the firm. *The Quarterly Journal of Economics,* 113(2), 387–432.

Ravasi, D. & Zattoni, A. (2006). Exploring the political side of board involvement in strategy: A study of mixed-ownership institutions. *Journal of Management Studies,* 43(8), 1671–702.

Raworth, K. (2017). *Doughnut Economics: Seven Ways to Think like a 21st Century Economist,* White River Junction, VT: Chelsea Green Publishing.

Regnér, P. (2003). Strategy creation in the periphery: Inductive versus deductive strategy making. *Journal of Management Studies,* 40(1), 57–82.

Rindova, V.P. (1999). What corporate boards have to do with strategy: A cognitive perspective. *Journal of Management Studies,* 36(7), 953–75.

Rouleau, L. (2013). Strategy-as-practice at a crossroads. *M@n@gement,* 16(5), 547–65.

Sarasvathy, S. D. (2001). Causation and effectuation: Toward a theoretical shift from economic inevitability to entrepreneurial contingency. *Academy of Management Review,* 26(2), 243–63.

Scherer, A. G., Baumann-Pauly, D. & Schneider, A. (2012). Democratizing corporate governance: Compensating for the democratic deficit of corporate political activity and corporate citizenship. *Business & Society,* 52(3), 473–514.

Schilling, M. A. (2018). The cognitive foundations of visionary strategy. *Strategy Science,* 3(1), 335–42.

Schoemaker, P. J. H., Heaton, S. & Teece, D. (2018). Innovation, dynamic capabilities, and leadership. *California Management Review,* 61(1), 15–42.

Schrage, M., Pring, B., Kiron, D. & Dickerson, D. (2021). *Leadership's Digital Transformation: Leading Purposefully in an Era of Context Collapse,* MIT Sloan Management Review and Cognizant Research Report.

Selznick, P. (1957). *Leadership in Administration*, New York: Harper and Row.

Simon, H. A. ([1947] 1976). *Administrative Behavior: A Study of Decision-Making Processes in Administrative Organization*, New York: Macmillan.

Simon, H. A. (1955), A behavioral model of rational choice. *Quarterly Journal of Economics*, 69(1), 99–118.

Simon, H. A. (1976), From substantive to procedural rationality. In S. Latsis, ed., *Method and Appraisal in Economics*, Cambridge: Cambridge University Press, pp. 129–48.

Sloan, A. P. (1963). *My Years with General Motors*, London: Sedgewick and Jackson.

Smircich, L. & Stubbart, C. (1985). Strategic management in an enacted world. *Academy of Management Review*, 10(4), 724–36.

Smith, A. (1776). *An Inquiry into the Wealth of Nations*, Hertfordshire: Wordsworth.

Snowden, D. J. & Boone, M. E. (2007). A leader's framework for decision making. *Harvard Business Review*, 85(11), 68–76.

Steiner, G. (1969). *Top Management Planning*, Englewood Cliffs, NJ: Prentice Hall.

Stiles, P. (2001). The impact of the board on strategy: An empirical examination. *Journal of Management Studies*, 38(5), 627–50.

Sundaramurthy, C. & Lewis, M. (2003). Control and collaboration: Paradoxes of governance. *Academy of Management Review*, 28(3), 397–415.

Teece, D. J. (2007). Explicating dynamic capabilities: The nature and micro-foundations of (sustainable) enterprise performance. *Strategic Management Journal*, 28(11), 1319–50.

Teece, D. J., Peteraf, M. & Leih, S. (2016). Dynamic capabilities and organizational agility: Risk, uncertainty, and strategy in the innovation economy, *California Management Review*, 58(4), 13–35.

Teece, D. J., Pisano, G. & Shuen, A. (1997). Dynamic capabilities and strategic management. *Strategic Management Journal*, 18(7), 509–33.

Thakor, A. V. & Quinn, R. E. (2013). *The Economics of Higher Purpose*, ECGI-Finance Working Paper 395.

Thomas, J. B., Watts Sussman, S. & Henderson, J. C. (2001). Understanding 'strategic learning': Linking organizational learning, knowledge management, and sensemaking. *Organization Science*, 12(3), 331–45.

Tirole, J. (2001). Corporate governance. *Econometrica*, 69(1), 1–35.

Tricker, R. I. (1994). *International Corporate Governance: Text, Readings and Cases*, Englewood Cliffs, NJ: Prentice Hall.

Turnbul, S. (2012). The limitations of corporate governance best practices. In T. Clarke and D. Branson, eds., T. Clarke and D. Branson, eds.,*Handbook of Corporate Governance*, London & Thousand Oaks, CA:: Sage, pp. 428–50.

Tushman, M. L. & O'Reilly, III, C. A. (1996). The ambidextrous organizations: Managing evolutionary and revolutionary change. *California Management Review*, 38(4), 8–30.

United Nations (2015). *Transforming Our World: The 2030 Agenda for Sustainable Development*, UN General Assembly.

Useem, M. (2012). The ascent of shareholder monitoring and strategic partnering. In T. Clarke and D. Branson, eds., T. Clarke and D. Branson, eds.,*The Sage Handbook of Corporate Governance*, London & Thousand Oaks, CA:: Sage, pp. 136–58.

Van den Steen, E. (2018). Strategy and the strategist: How it matters who develops the strategy. *Management Science*, 64(10), 4533–51.

Van der Heijden, K. (1996). *Scenarios: The Art of Strategic Conversation*, Chichester: Wiley.

Van Ees, H., Bood, R. P. & Postma, T. J. B. M. (2019). The strategy role of the board revisited. Paper presented at the European Academy of Management Conference, Lisbon.

Van Ees, H., Gabrielsson, J. & Huse, M. (2009). Toward a behavioral theory of boards and corporate governance. *Corporate Governance: An International Review*, 17(3), 307–19.

Wack, P. (1985). Scenarios: Uncharted waters ahead. *Harvard Business Review*, 63(5), 73–90.

Walls, J. L. & Hoffman, A. J. (2013). Exceptional boards: Environmental experience and positive deviance from institutional norms. *Journal of Organizational Behavior*, 34(2), 253–71.

Weick, K. E. (1979). *The Social Psychology of Organizing*, New York: Random House.

Williamson, O. E. (1985). *The Economic Institutions of Capitalism*, New York: Free Press.

Williamson, O. E. (1996). *The Mechanisms of Governance*. New York: Oxford University Press.

Wiltbank, R., Dew, N., Read, S. & Sarasvathy, S. D. (2006). What to do next? The case for non-predictive strategy. *Strategic Management Journal*, 27(10), 981–98.

Whittington, R. (1993). *What Is Strategy and Does It Matter?* London: Thomson Learning.

Whittington, R. (1996). Strategy as practice. *Long Range Planning*, 29(5), 731–5.

Whittington, R., Cailluet, L. & Yakis-Douglas, B. (2011). Opening strategy: Evolution of a precarious profession. *British Journal of Management*, 22(3), 531–44.

Whittington, R., Molloy, E., Mayer, M. & Smith, A. (2006). Practices of strategising/organising: Broadening strategy work and skills. *Long Range Planning*, 39(6), 615–29.

Younger, R., Mayer, C. & Eccles, R. G. (2020). *Enacting Purpose within the Modern Corporation: A Framework for Boards of Directors*. Downloaded December 2020 from Enactingpurpose.org: www.enactingpurpose.org/assets/enacting-purpose-initiative–eu-report-august-2020.pdf.

Zahra, S. A. & Filatotchev, I. (2004). Governance of entrepreneurial threshold firm: A knowledge-based perspective, *Journal of Management Studies*, 41 (5), 885–98.

Zahra, S. A. & Pearce, J. A. (1989). Boards of directors and corporate financial performance: A review and integrative model. *Journal of Management*, 15 (2), 291–334.

Zattoni, A., Gnan, L. & Huse, M. (2015). Does family involvement influence firm performance? Exploring the mediating effects of board processes and tasks. *Journal of Management*, 41(4), 1214–43.

Zeitoun, H., Osterloh, M. & Frey, B. (2014). Learning from ancient Athens: Demarchy and corporate governance. *The Academy of Management Perspectives*, 28(1), 1–14.

Zingales, L. (2000). In search of new foundations. *The Journal of Finance*, 55 (4), 1623–53.

Cambridge Elements ☰

Corporate Governance

Thomas Clarke

UTS Business School, University of Technology Sydney

Thomas Clarke is Professor of Corporate Governance at the UTS Business School of the University of Technology Sydney. His work focuses on the institutional diversity of corporate governance and his most recent book is *International Corporate Governance* (Second Edition 2017). He is interested in questions about the purposes of the corporation, and the convergence of the concerns of corporate governance and corporate sustainability.

About the series

The series Elements in Corporate Governance focuses on the significant emerging field of corporate governance. Authoritative, lively and compelling analyses include expert surveys of the foundations of the discipline, original insights into controversial debates, frontier developments and masterclasses on key issues. Its areas of interest include empirical studies of corporate governance in practice, regional institutional diversity, emerging fields, key problems and core theoretical perspectives.

Cambridge Elements $\equiv$

Corporate Governance

Elements in the series

Printed in the United States
by Baker & Taylor Publisher Services